Getting Ready for Fifth Grade

In fourth grade, your child learned how to apply basic reading skills to other areas of study. Fourth graders also began connecting the abstract to the concrete. Your fourth-grade graduate may be able to

- identify and discuss parts of speech.
- read and discuss different writing genres (mystery, nonfiction, fantasy, myths, legends, autobiographies, historical fiction, poetry).
- know how and when to use the dictionary, glossary, and other resource materials.
- classify sentences as declarative (statements), interrogative (questions), exclamatory (exclamation), or commands.
- provide synonyms, antonyms, and homonyms for given words.
- identify cause and effect.
- use context clues to decode unfamiliar vocabulary.
- recognize prefixes, suffixes, and roots of English words.
- add and subtract fractions and decimals.
- identify patterns in multiplication and division sentences.
- multiply and divide by multidigit numbers.
- compute area and perimeter.
- explore percentages and their relationship to fractions and decimals.

Grade 5 Skills

Fifth-grade students start assuming responsibility for their learning. Fifth graders seek ways of incorporating their growing need to be social with classroom learning experiences, and they enjoy chances for cooperative study. By the end of the fifth grade, your child may be able to

- use synonyms, antonyms, homophones, and analogies to build vocabulary.
- recognize and apply all parts of speech.
- incorporate suspense, dialogue, and figurative language into writing.
- edit writing from knowledge of spelling, punctuation, and grammar and usage.
- form analogies, similes, and metaphors to establish relationships.
- use deductive reasoning to make predictions and inferences in literature.
- expand personal writing in the form of letters, essays, and journal entries.
- condense learning material through note taking, outlines, and summaries.
- use and discuss symbolism and personification (attributing human characteristics to animals or objects) in writing and literature.
- identify, measure, and convert units of length, capacity, and mass in customary and metric units.
- perform operations accurately using whole numbers, fractions, and decimals.
- determine the perimeter of polygons and the area of squares and rectangles.

How You Can Help

You can help prepare your child for fifth grade by making this Summer Vacation™ book a regular part of your daily routine. Work with your child to construct the weather station, and help with additional research and written activities. The Summer Vacation™ book is designed to help your child retain the skills that he or she developed in fourth grade and to prepare him or her for the challenges of fifth grade.

VOCABULARY QUIZ

Circle the word that matches the definition.

1. **accept**   to take or receive something offered
   except

2. **affect**   consequence, that which is produced by some cause
   effect

3. **air**   one who inherits
   heir

4. **choral**   related to a chorus or choir
   coral

5. **cite**   the power of seeing
   sight

Journal

NOTE: If you need more room, use a blank sheet of paper.

Listening to music makes us feel good. What are some of
your favorite songs and why are they your favorites?

_____

_____

_____

PLACE VALUE

Write the correct number or fill in the correct number of tally marks in each place.

Example

1,000,000s	100,000s	10,000s	1,000s	100s	10s	1s
//	////	卌 ///	/	///	//	卌 /

Answer: 2,481,326

1.

1,000,000s	100,000s	10,000s	1,000s	100s	10s	1s

Answer: 8,211,555

2.

1,000,000s	100,000s	10,000s	1,000s	100s	10s	1s
////	卌 ////	//	卌 //	卌 //	///	卌 ///

Answer: _____

3.

1,000,000s	100,000s	10,000s	1,000s	100s	10s	1s
	卌 ////	卌 ///	卌 ////		/	/

Answer: _____

4.

1,000,000s	100,000s	10,000s	1,000s	100s	10s	1s

Answer: 3,001,992

5.

1,000,000s	100,000s	10,000s	1,000s	100s	10s	1s

Answer: 8,729,818

6.

1,000,000s	100,000s	10,000s	1,000s	100s	10s	1s
卌 /	卌 ////			卌 /		////

Answer: _____

7.

1,000,000s	100,000s	10,000s	1,000s	100s	10s	1s
卌	卌 //	//	卌 /	////	////	卌 //

Answer: _____

8.

1,000,000s	100,000s	10,000s	1,000s	100s	10s	1s

Answer: 9,116,533

Journal

NOTE: If you need more room, use a blank sheet of paper.

TUESDAY

This summer, I hope to do the following fun things:

_____
_____
_____
_____
_____
_____
_____
_____
_____

MEGA MATH

Find values for each shape and solve the equations.

$\triangle = 4$ $\bullet = ?$ $\blacksquare = ?$

$\bullet\bullet = \triangle\triangle\triangle$

$\triangle\triangle\triangle\triangle \quad \bullet\bullet\bullet\bullet = \blacksquare\blacksquare\blacksquare$

$\blacksquare\blacksquare\bullet\triangle = ?$

Recipes

Parental supervision is recommended.

GOOP!
Otherwise Known As Cool Stuff!

Ingredients:
cornstarch
water

Equipment:
container
water
stirrer
measuring spoon
measuring cup

Directions:
Mix 1/2 cup of cornstarch with 1 teaspoon of water. Stir. If too crumbly, add more water. The substance should appear liquidy on top. Poke it and see! Put a little in your hand and then squeeze it tightly, open your hand. What happened to the substance?

Games   Math in the Box

10	+		+		−		+

=	10 + innings in baseball + dwarfs in Snow White - quarters in football + planets	−
+	=	−
	the value of 1 quarter, 2 dimes and 3 pennies	stripes on U.S. flag
−	+	+
	minutes in 2 hours	1st 2-digit birthday
+	-	−
	dinosaurs on the planet	dozen
	+	+
	sides on a stop sign	toes
−	-	=
	continents + feet in a yard - seconds in a minute + thumbs -	26

	+		−		+		−	26

- Will this come out right?
- Adding and subtracting as you go around, see if you get the same numbers as shown in the two corners!

THE MYSTERY OF THE LOST TIME CAPSULE

Chapter 1

On a warm, pleasant Saturday in June, the people of Middletown gathered at the town square. Cody, Peyton and Klugh, the town's youngest and most curious detectives, made their way through the noisy crowd. Cody's pet ferret, Misjiff, ran along side.

"I wonder what's going on," Cody said to his friends. "It looks like the mayor is going to speak."

The mayor of Middletown stood on the bandstand and called the crowd to order. "Next Saturday our town will celebrate its bicentennial," he said. "Middletown will be 200 years old!" The crowd cheered.

"Today," the mayor continued, "we are announcing a special contest. One hundred years ago, during the town's centennial celebration, a time capsule was buried. It is said to be buried in the oldest building in Middletown. An anonymous donor has offered a $1,000 reward to the person who finds this time capsule. The winner will be declared at next Saturday's festival. Good luck and happy hunting!"

Cody and his friends loved adventure, and searching for the time capsule sounded like a good one. "Did you hear that, guys?" Cody asked. "This sounds like just the mystery we've been looking for!"

"What's a time capsule?" Peyton asked. Peyton was the levelheaded one who thought things through.

Cody thought a moment. "The way I understand it, people put special stuff in a box and bury it in a special place. It's supposed to show what a place or a group of people was like during a certain time period."

"What kind of stuff do they put in it?" asked Klugh, who loved to listen for clues and solve mysteries.

"Oh, I don't know," said Cody. "Old coins, town papers, maybe newspapers, and photographs."

"Old coins could be very valuable," Peyton said. "Remember in history class when Ms. Carson said coins were made of real gold and silver in the old days?"

"Wow!" said Klugh. "There could be a real treasure in the time capsule!"

"Since the Cherokee Indians lived in this area first, maybe they put something special in the time capsule, too," Cody said.

"Cool," Peyton said. "It's like history in a box."

"If we win the $1,000, we can all go to that science camp Ms. Carson told us about," said Klugh. The three friends shook hands.

"We're in this together," they said.

"Chee, chee, chee," chattered Misjiff.

ACTIVITY 1

Reading Comprehension—Story Map

Fill in the map to show important ideas in the story.

Setting

Where does this story take place?

_____

_____

_____

Characters

Who are the main characters in the story?

_____

_____

_____

Problem

What problem do the characters decide to solve?

_____

_____

_____

Plot

What happens in this chapter?

_____

_____

_____

Question and Answer

This technical innovation, when hooked up to your TV or computer, can play music and movies all in the same package.

What is it?

FACTOID

The human body contains approximately 12 pints (6 liters) of blood for an adult male and 9 pints (4 liters) for an adult female.

Logic Problems

Which comes next?

Can you solve the relationship between the numbers and the words? What would come next?

1 Hippo

2 Hat

3 Cat

4 Leaf

5 Scarf

6 Cars

7 Stars

8 Dive

9 Fan

10 ?

Dog
Tent
Ball
Umbrella

Weird Science

Smooth Moves With Marbles

Feel the difference that ball bearings make when you need to move a heavy load.

You will need: 20 to 30 marbles, two or three heavy books, pen, scissors, a large round plastic tub that you can cut up (such as for sherbet or frozen non-dairy topping), smooth floor or kitchen counter and six or more round pencils (not flat-sided)

Straight Moves:

- Stack the books one on top of the other on the counter or smooth floor and then push them along with your hands; the resistance that you feel is caused by the friction between the book's cover and the counter.
- Draw a line around the outside of the plastic tub, about half an inch down from the rim. Using scissors, carefully poke a hole into the tub on the line, then cut all the way around, so that you end up with a narrow ring. (The ring must be narrower than the marble diameters.)
- Place the ring on the counter and fill it with the marbles, then place the stack of books on top of the filled ring.
- Push the stack again, using your fingertips to keep the ring of marbles centered under the books. The stack will glide across the counter with very little effort.

SPIN

Easy Spins:

- With just the books, try pushing one corner of the stack to spin it on the counter or floor. How far around does one push make it rotate?
- Place the books on the ring of marbles, and give the corner a push. See how easily it turns—just guide it to keep it centered on the ring.

Moving with Rollers:

- Line up all the pencils side by side on the counter and then lay a book on top. Push the books along. If the books move off the pencils, take a pencil from one side and add it to the far side, to keep the books rolling.

What's Happening:

When you push on just the books, the entire surface of the book cover is in contact with the counter. This creates friction at every point on the surface. Using the marbles as a set of ball bearings, the bottom book only touches the topmost bit of each marble, and the spherical surfaces are free to roll. The books slide easily over the marbles, and the marbles slide easily over the counter. Much less friction means much less effort required to make the stack slide or spin.

Try the experiment again, using tiny silver sugar balls (sold with cake decorations and candles). Will they hold the same weight as the marbles? The rolling pencils do the same job that rolling logs did for ancient peoples who needed to move huge stones (perhaps at Stonehenge or the Pyramids).

Remember to use the Scientific Method!

1) Make your hypothesis.
2) Record your observations.
3) Draw your conclusions.

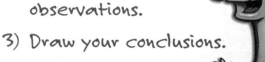

AVERAGING

To find the average for each group, add the numbers together and divide by the total amount of numbers in each group.

Example: 3, 9, 12, 12 = 3 + 9 + 12 + 12 = 36 ÷ 4 = 9
9 is the average

1. 5, 10, 15

Average = _____

2. 7, 8, 45, 20

Average = _____

3. 2, 2, 20

Average = _____

4. 5, 5, 5, 5

Average = _____

5. 1, 2, 3, 4

Average = _____

6. 100, 10, 10

Average = _____

7. 30, 20, 49

Average = _____

8. 7, 2, 9, 10

Average = _____

FRIDAY

Can you get from (in)side to out(doors)?

Use compound words to create path
from start to finish.
(Example: ice + box = icebox then,
box + car = boxcar)

GLASS	BROKEN	STRING	STRONG	WORK	DOWN	THERE	SEAT
IN	OUT	TOWER	QUART	HOLD	HOUSE	LIGHT	SIDE
TIME	FRONT	END	HERE	OVER	FOR	TIME	IN
BUS	WASH	HIGH	WOOD	BOARD	GOOD	GOAL	TIME
DOORS	OUT	DROP	OUT	WALK	OUT	PLANE	HERE
OVER	ADD	BACK	RUN	SEE	SIDE	DARK	NIGHT
SPOT	ONE	SWEPT	WIND	DOWN	SHOW	AHEAD	WIND
PASS	FREE	ON	SLOW	SITE	DANGER	NOW	LIGHT

START

FINISH

CROSSWORD

Can you guess the relationship?

	1		3

2 T I M E Z O N E S

Across:
2. Eastern, central, mountain
4. Bundt, carrot, short
6. Ottoman, chaise-lounge, armoire
8. Brooklyn, Golden Gate, Mackinaw
9. Autumn, spring, winter

Down:
1. New, full, crescent, harvest
3. Heels, wingtips, sandals
4. Brasilia, London, Moscow
5. Powdered, jelly, cruller
7. Revolutionary, Civil, 1812

JOINING WORDS

and, but, or, because, when, after, so

Fill in the blank with the correct joining word.

1. I like rainy days _____ I like the sound the rain makes.

2. You have a choice of finishing your homework _____ cleaning your room.

3. My friend is coming over _____ she goes to the dentist.

4. He borrowed a dollar _____ he could buy a newspaper.

5. My mom loves spinach, _____ my dad hates it.

6. I will get a reward _____ I get a good report card.

Make a Weather Station:
How's the Weather?

Adult supervision is recommended.

Introduction to the Project

During the next 12 weeks, your child will have the opportunity to learn about weather by building a weather station. The simple devices he or she makes will help teach the basic concepts of meteorology, including the measurement of temperature, cloud type, wind direction and speed, rainfall, air pressure, and humidity. Your child also will keep a weather log, a process that emphasizes the importance of good data collection. The skills of observation and careful recording are critical to the scientific method. Weather logs will also help your child read, analyze and interpret data.

Although none of the activities involve hazardous materials, adult supervision is recommended. An explanation of each device appears with its instructions; however, you may need to expand or supplement this information with discussion and answer any questions your child may have. You can find general weather information at http://kids.earth.nasa.gov and www.nssl.noaa.gov/edu.

Master Materials List

cardboard

3 clear glass or plastic jars, at least 5 in. (12.7 cm) tall

3 coffee can lids (or similar soft plastic lids)

scissors

water

ice cubes

6 discarded compact discs or CD-ROMs (can also use shells, nails or bolts)

3 craft sticks, each 18 in. (45.7 cm) long

dime

dowel or tree branch, 18 in. (45.7 cm)

fishing line, 108–120 in. (274.3–304.8 cm)

a few drops of food coloring

glue

3 or 4 strands of human hair

marker

metal pan or tray

modeling clay

notebook or binder with $8 \frac{1}{2}$ in. × 11 in. (21.6 cm × 27.9 cm) paper

$8 \frac{1}{2}$ in. × 11 in. (21.6 cm × 27.9 cm) paper

5 paper cups, 3 oz. (85 g) each

hole punch

3 pencils with erasers

2 plastic bags

6 plastic straws (one must be clear)

2 pushpins (not thumbtacks)

ruler

sand or gravel

shovel

2 soft-drink bottles

stapler

2 stones

2 straight pins

thermometer

waterproof tape, such as duct tape or electrical tape

wood, thick cardboard, or foam, 10 in. × 4 in. (25.4 cm × 10.2 cm)

weatherproof box, 24 in. × 24 in. × 18 in. (61 cm × 61 cm × 45.7 cm)

Materials

a weatherproof box, about 24 in. × 24 in. × 18 in.
   (61 cm × 61 cm × 45.7 cm)

Directions

1. This box will make a safe, sturdy place
   to store your weather tools. If you wish,
   decorate the box.

2. Find a place for the box on the north
   side of your house if you can, or put
   it in a shady spot so that it won't be
   affected by sunlight. Check with an
   adult to see whether the place you
   have chosen is all right.

3. Place the box on its side so that the
   opening, or top, is now on the side.
   You will be making tools to attach
   to this box. This will be your
   weather station.

Meteorology is the study of weather.
Meteorologists study weather conditions
and changes. One of the most important
things meteorologists do is forecast the
weather. They use tools to measure how
warm the air is, how dry it is, and how
quickly and in what direction it is moving.
These measurements are clues to the type
and intensity of weather we can experience.

For this project, you will be taking weather
measurements. You will make the tools
needed to take the measurements. As you
build each tool, you will learn some of the
vocabulary meteorologists use and how
the tools work. In order for these tools to
measure the weather, they must remain
outside *in* the weather.

**Place quotation marks around the words of
the speaker for each sentence.**

Example: "How are you feeling?" asked the doctor.

1. She screamed, Get out of the way!

2. What did you say? asked the teacher.

3. The waiter asked, What type of salad dressing would you like?

4. Turn up the radio! shouted Bobby.

5. When will we be there? asked the children.

6. Grandma asked, Would you like some tea?

7. Abby's mother reminded her, Don't forget your sunscreen.

8. Do you want to play baseball? asked Susan.

Journal

NOTE: If you need more room, use a blank sheet of paper.

Our family is very important in our lives. Describe
something you did this week with someone in your family.

_____

_____

_____

_____

MULTIPLICATION

Solve the equations below.

1.　　416
　　x　88

2.　　336
　　x　24

3.　　510
　　x　50

4.　　921
　　x　82

5.　　186
　　x　15

6.　　722
　　x　63

7.　　649
　　x　42

8.　　249
　　x　10

9.　　247
　　x　39

Journal

NOTE: If you need more room, use a blank sheet of paper.

Finish this story:

I was in the basement looking for my in-line skates and I saw a strange shadow under the staircase. Imagine my suprise when I saw that it was... _____

_____

_____

_____

_____

_____

_____

_____

_____

MEGA MATH

Find values for each shape and solve the equations.

▲ = ?   ● = ?   ■ = 5

● ■ = ▲ ▲

▲ ▲ ▲ ▲ ▲ = ■ ■ ■ ■

● x ▲ + ■ = ?

20

Recipes

Parental supervision is recommended.

Scream For Ice Cream

Ingredients:

1 beaten egg
1 cup heavy cream
1 cup light cream
1/2 cup sugar
1 tsp vanilla extract

Directions:

Mix ingredients and place in smaller can. Put the lid on. Seal lid on with duct tape. Place small can into larger can. Pack ice and salt around smaller can. Seal lid onto larger can with duct tape. Roll the can back and forth with a friend for about 20 minutes. Now you've got ice cream!

Equipment:

large coffee can with lid
small coffee can with lid
duct tape
1 cup rock salt
ice

Games   Memory Magazine

- Begin by cutting out pictures from old magazines.
- Glue them on cardboard creating a poster. Each person makes their own poster. Then take turns, showing the others your poster (allow them to look at it for 3 minutes). Then cover it up.
- Have them write down everything they saw on your poster.
- Now have that person hold up their poster.
- Repeat until all have had a turn.
- The one who remembers the most wins!

THE MYSTERY OF THE LOST TIME CAPSULE

Chapter 2

Later that afternoon Cody, Peyton and Klugh met in the town square to begin their search for the time capsule. "We've got to have a plan," said Cody. "Every good detective has a plan!"

"Since we're in the center of town, let's start here," Peyton suggested. She was not the only one who had that same idea. Several other residents, including Professor Smith, who taught history at Middletown University, were also gathered at the town square.

Cody and his team set out from the grassy square, noticing the dates etched into the old red brick library, 1898, and the town hall, 1850. When they came to the Morning Star Cafe, Klugh sat down on the bench outside the cafe's purple door. Misjiff jumped up in his lap.

"Remember how Ms. Carson said that pioneer towns often sprang up along rivers?" said Klugh. "I think we should head down by the river and nose around a little."

"Not me," said Peyton. "The old Warner place is down there, and I'm not going near it. Mr. Warner's a strange old man."

"He never comes into town," Cody said. "And he never gives out treats at Halloween."

"See? He hates kids," said Peyton.

"His house couldn't be the oldest anyhow," Cody said. "It has aluminum siding on it, and I'm pretty sure the settlers didn't have siding," he laughed.

"Let's walk down there anyhow," urged Klugh. "We might find valuable clues."

"Well, all right," Peyton said, "but I'm not getting too close."

As they neared Mr. Warner's house, they stumbled over a stone wall covered with overgrown weeds. It seemed to go around the entire property. The part they could see was made of large, flat stones and looked very old. Cody and Klugh bent down to take a closer look, while Peyton kept an eye on the house.

"I-I-I don't like this," Peyton stammered, and then she jumped in fear. Cody and Klugh looked up just in time to see a dark figure moving past the front window.

WEDNESDAY

Skill: Word Study—Word Detective

How many three- and four-letter words can you find in *bicentennial*? Write your words in the columns below. Use a dictionary to check the spelling of your words.

B I C E N T E N N I A L

3 letters

_____

_____

_____

_____

_____

_____

_____

_____

_____

_____

_____

_____

4 letters

_____

_____

_____

_____

_____

_____

_____

_____

_____

_____

_____

_____

Question and Answer

The smallest of its kind were called obelas. They were used in Greece and were about the same size as a sunflower seed.

What were they?

FACTOID

John Glenn is an American astronaut who flew on Friendship 7, February 20, 1962, and returned to space aboard the space shuttle Discovery on October 29, 1998, at the age of 77.

Logic Problems

Which comes next?

Can you solve the relationship between the numbers and the words? What would come next?

1	Egg	6	Xylophone
2	Ostrich	7	Nail
3	Elephant	8	Train
4	Rat	9	Ear
5	Eel	10	?

Nuts
Ball
Candy
Dolphin

Weird Science

Ink Chemistry

We write with different kinds of pens and markers every day, but do you know what's really inside them? Why are some colors washable and others definitely not? Break down some inks and mix up some others to find out the real message.

You will need: permanent ink markers (highlighters in orange and purple, felt-tip pens in colors such as black and brown), empty clean can (large coffee can is good, but smaller will work) rubber bands, old white T-shirt, baking soda, water, eyedropper or craftsticks, milk, lemon juice, sliced bread (white is best), toaster, sugar, paper, pencil

Black Ink Really Isn't:

• Spread part of the T-shirt over the opening of the can. Stretch a rubber band over the cloth to hold it flat and tight.

• Use the markers to draw your name, a shape, or a design on the stretched fabric. Lots of thin lines will work better than broad colored-in sections.

• Mix a teaspoon of baking soda into 1/4 cup water; stir.

• Use an eyedropper or craftstick to scoop up a few drops of the water mixture, and let them drip onto the lines of the design. The extra liquid will drip into the can; you can throw that away when you're done.

• What do you see happening? What is in the black, brown, orange and purple inks? Try other marker brands, too.

• If you want, draw more designs on your shirt and add the water mixture drops. Let it dry and wear it.

Disappearing Inks:

• Dip a craftstick into water and dribble your initials, a circle, or another pattern onto a slice of plain bread. Toast it in the toaster on dark. What do you see?

• Try "writing" on other bread slices using milk or lemon juice. Toast them. Which liquid makes the best "ink?"

• Use milk, lemon juice, or a little sugar in water to write on paper. Let the paper dry, then lightly rub the side of a pencil over the places where you wrote. What happens?

Separating the black (or other) ink into two or more colors is called chromatography. It depends on a chemical reaction taking place. Making the "invisible ink" visible took mechanical energy, and a contrasting material (graphite). Some invisible inks also show up when heated due to a thermal reaction.

Ink chemists try thousands of chemical combinations to create not only new colors, but also new properties such as permanent, washable, dry-erase, erasable, and color-changing.

Try making your own inks from squashed berries, flowers or vegetables. How do they look wet or dry? Are they very dark? Do they work differently if you microwave them in some water first?

Remember to use the Scientific Method!

1) Make your hypothesis.

2) Record your observations.

3) Draw your conclusions.

DECIMALS

Fill in the blank with the correct math symbol to compare each group of decimals. > means greater than and < means less than.

1. .98 ____ .72

2. .21 ____ .66

3. .11 ____ .29

4. .04 ____ .14

5. .06 ____ .04

6. .49 ____ .88

7. .62 ____ .58

8. .09 ____ .10

FRIDAY

Can you guide the ship safely back to port?

Use compound words to create path from start to finish.
(Example: ice + box = icebox then, box + car = boxcar)

START →

BACK	FLAG	OLD	BIG	TIRE	GOING	AGAINST	TOP
DOOR	HANDLE	BAR	REST	FORM	SIDE	BLUE	DOG
WEST	LEFT	BELL	CHIME	RED	ZONE	TRAIN	ZONE
SHIP	FRIEND	BOY	HARD	COLD	WATER	FALL	OUT
YARD	BOAT	GIRL	WORK	DAY	BREAK	OUT	BACK
STICK	LESS	SEAL	PIECE	SUN	QUICK	WALK	BOARD
PIN	BALL	GAME	TIME	RUN	LINE	OVER	PASS
CAT	BROWN	MICE	HOT	AIR	TREE	HEAT	PORT

FINISH

CROSSWORD

Can you guess the relationship?

Across:

4. Asia, Australia, Antarctica

7. Left, straight, west

9. Square, parallelogram, rhombus

10. Curling, rugby, jai alai

Down:

1. Cherokee, Inuit, Ojibwa

2. Cotton, rayon, polyester

3. Democracy, Communism, monarchy

5. Glass, tin cans, plastic, newspapers

6. Ohio, Mississippi, Rio Grande

8. Picasso, Cezanne, Renoir

PALINDROMES

SATURDAY

Palindromes are words or sentences that are spelled the same forward or backward.

Example: dad

Write the correct palindrome for each statement below.

1. The woman you call mother. _____

2. The day before Christmas is Christmas_____.

3. We eat lunch at 12:00 p.m. _____

4. A baby wears this when it eats. _____

5. Past tense verb for do. _____

6. Three-letter word people say when they are surprised or impressed.

_____

Make a Weather Station:
Keeping a Weather Journal
Adult supervision is recommended.

Meteorologists keep daily records of the temperature. By comparing today's temperature to temperatures for this date in the past, a meteorologist can say whether today is warmer or cooler than normal.

In the same way, meteorologists measure wind speed and determine the direction in which the wind is blowing. Meteorologists also measure *air pressure* (the force or weight of the air as it presses down on Earth), *humidity* (how moist the air is), and *precipitation* (rain, sleet, hail or snow) to help them make forecasts. For example, if records from earlier years showed that falling air pressure was followed by a cloudy or rainy day, what might you predict when your instruments show that air pressure has begun to fall?

During this project you will learn that keeping good records is one of the most important responsibilities that a scientist has.

Materials
notebook or binder with 8 $\frac{1}{2}$ in. × 11 in. (21.6 cm × 27.9 cm) paper

Date	Time	Temperature	Sky	Wind Direction	Wind Speed	Rain	Humidity	Air Pressure
June 16	9:10 A.M.	warm	sunny		light	none	low	
June 17	9:15 A.M.	warm	partly cloudy		light	none	medium	
June 18	8:45 A.M.	warm	cloudy		medium	none	high	
June 19	9:30 A.M.	cool	cloudy		light	light	high	
June 20	9:40 A.M.	warm	partly cloudy		light	light	medium	
June 21	9:44 A.M.	warm	sunny		light	none	low	

Directions

1. Make several forms like the one shown on the previous page. On your paper, make headings for each column as shown.

2. Record a weather observation at least once a day. Be careful not to miss a day. Complete records are the key to understanding weather.

3. Make your observations at about the same time every day. Doing so makes it easier to compare changes.

4. For now, just use the words *hot, warm* or *cool* for temperature, *high, medium* or *low* for humidity, and *light* or *heavy* for rain. Leave "Wind Direction" and "Air Pressure" blank. As you build your weather instruments, you will enter more precise data.

5. At the end of a week, look at your record. What trends do you see?

_____

_____

_____

_____

Extension

Weather and *climate* are not the same thing. Use a dictionary or an encyclopedia to find out the difference between the two terms. Write your findings on the lines below. Include descriptions of your area's weather and climate.

_____

_____

_____

_____

_____

_____

ANALOGIES

Analogies compare how things relate to each other. Match the groups of words together to make the correct analogies.

1. Glove is to baseball as

2. Hat is to head as

3. Tomato is to spaghetti sauce as

4. Nephew is to uncle as

5. Hair is to human as

6. Page is to book as

7. Corn crop is to farmer as

8. Hammer is to tool belt as

a. shoe is to foot

b. niece is to aunt

c. charm is to bracelet

d. shin pad is to soccer

e. letter is to alphabet

f. lemon is to lemonade

g. article is to newspaper journalist

h. fur is to animal

Journal

NOTE: If you need more room, use a blank sheet of paper.

Having keys to the house is a responsibility that kids have as they get older. What are you entrusted to do around the house that makes you feel responsible?

_____

_____

_____

MONEY STORY PROBLEMS

Solve the problems using addition, subtraction, multiplication and division.

1. You received $20.00 for your birthday. You bought a CD for $14.99 with your birthday money. How much change did you get back?

_____

2. Your family of four went to a professional baseball game. The tickets cost $21.00 each. All four of you ate a hot dog and a soda pop. Hot dogs cost $2.00 each and soda pop cost $1.00 each. How much money did your family spend at the baseball game?

_____

3. You earned $14.50 selling lemonade at your lemonade stand. You charged $.50 for each glass of lemonade. How many glasses of lemonade did you sell?

_____

Journal

NOTE: If you need more room, use a blank sheet of paper.

What would you like to be when you grow up? Why?

_____

_____

_____

_____

_____

_____

_____

_____

_____

MEGA MATH

Find values for each shape and solve the equations.

$$\triangle = ? \qquad \bullet = ? \qquad \blacksquare = 4$$

$$\blacksquare \ \blacksquare \ \bullet = \triangle$$

$$\triangle \ \bullet = \blacksquare \ \blacksquare \ \blacksquare$$

$$\frac{\triangle \ \blacksquare}{\bullet} = 7$$

Parental supervision is recommended.

"Moldy" Bagels

Ingredients:

1/2 dozen plain bagels
1 can of tomato or pizza sauce
1 pkg. shredded Mozzarella
4 tablespoons grated Parmesan cheese
green food coloring

Equipment:

bowl
aluminum foil
cookie sheet
spoon
plastic wrap

Directions:

Cut bagels in half so you have two separate pieces. Cover the cookie sheet with aluminum foil and place the bagels on them (cut side up). With your spoon, spread the sauce on top and add a layer of the Mozzarella cheese on top. Now, pour the Parmesan cheese into a small bowl. Add ten drops of the green food coloring. Cover your hand in the plastic wrap and mix the cheese up with the food coloring.

Broil the bagels in the oven until the cheese begins to turn brown. When they're done, take the bagels out and let them cool for about two minutes. Now sprinkle your green "moldy" cheese on top. Gross and satisfying!

Games   The Letter Game

To be played while traveling in a car or walking along the street.

- The object is to be the first one to complete the alphabet using letters you see in sequence.

- You can get your letters from license plates, billboards or traffic signs.

- You must declare when you find a letter and make it known to your opponent(s).

- You must use your letters in sequence (you may not use letters out of turn).

- The first one to finish the alphabet wins!

THE MYSTERY OF THE LOST TIME CAPSULE

Chapter 3

"Calm down, Peyton," Cody said. He pointed to the giant oak tree next to the house. "It was just that old tree swaying in the wind."

"I know I saw someone in that front window," she said.

"You're just worried about Mr. Warner," Klugh said. "Come on and help us examine this old stone wall."

Cody, Klugh and Peyton began pulling back the weeds that had grown up around the wall. Misjiff zoomed around his friends, up and over the wall, and back again.

The amateur detectives carefully studied the rocks that made up the wall. "Look over here," Klugh called. He showed them the beginning of a wide stone path leading up to the little house.

The stones were worn down from years of use. Some had deep grooves, showing evidence of many comings and goings.

"These stones are pretty old," Cody said.

"Ancient," said Klugh.

"Are you thinking what I'm thinking?" Peyton asked.

"I'm thinking this path could be leading us to the oldest house in Middletown," Cody said. "And maybe a buried time capsule."

"If the pioneers built here first, how come the professor and the others aren't looking here?"

"They're thinking what we first thought—that the center of town was where it all began," said Klugh. "But Ms. Carson said that towns grew up where people could have easy transportation for travel and trade."

"Klugh's right," Cody said. "I'll bet that the first settlers built their homes at the bend in the river. Right here!"

"Let's go behind the house," said Klugh. "There might be a path that leads to the river. That would tell us a lot."

"I'm not going back there," said Peyton. "Who knows what Mr. Warner has in his back yard?"

Cody grabbed Peyton's hand and said, "Come on. There's nothing to be afraid of."

They crept toward the rear of the house. Misjiff ran along, sniffing and chattering.

Suddenly they heard the front door open and a deep voice boomed, "What do you kids want?"

Cody, Klugh and Peyton froze in their tracks.

WEDNESDAY

Skill: Sequence of Events

Here is a list of events that happened in this chapter.
Number them in the correct order.

☐ Klugh finds the remains of an old stone path.

☐ Cody tells Peyton that the shadow was the oak tree moving.

☐ A deep voice asks what the kids want.

☐ Cody, Klugh and Peyton pull back weeds around the stone wall.

☐ Cody, Klugh and Peyton walk toward the back yard of the Warner house.

☐ Klugh remembers that towns often began near rivers.

Question and Answer

These tiny animals suck the blood out of human beings and other organisms, but at one point in time doctors prescribed them as a cure for patients!

What are they?

FACTOID

There are three separate branches of government in America—the Executive branch, the Judicial branch and the Legislative branch. Each branch receives its authority from the Constitution. The founding fathers designed this system of "checks and balances" so that no single branch would become too powerful.

Logic Problems

Which comes next?

Can you solve the relationship between the numbers and the words? What would come next?

1	Log	6	Ice
2	Cat	7	Grill
3	Tiger	8	Chief
4	Fish	9	Ball
5	Lion	10	?

Fog
Desk
Letter
Paper

Weird Science

Wheels Do More Than Roll

You know that it's easy to move heavy stuff when you have a cart or a wagon, but wheels help carry loads in many other ways. Make a people-powered toy elevator and a tabletop delivery system that both use spinning parts for useful work.

You will need: plastic straws, scissors, a wooden ruler, a chair or countertop, a thread spool, string or yarn, a tiny box or basket with handles, masking tape, 2 toilet paper tubes, 2 long pencils, paper (sheets or a roll), 6 rubber bands, a table, and 2 chairs

Going Up:

* Cut a straw in half. Tape one piece across the ruler near the end. Tape the ruler to a countertop or top of a chair. Thread a piece of yarn or string about 18 inches (46 cm) long through the straw and let it hang.

* Wrap a piece of masking tape around the thread spool. Slide another straw half through the spool. Run one end of the yarn from the ruler's straw through the spool's straw, and tie both yarn ends together.

* Cut another piece of yarn a little more than twice the height of the spool from the floor. Run it up and over the spool. Tie one end to the handle of the basket, or through holes punched in the sides of the box.

* Load the box with a toy, candy, etc., and pull on the free end of the yarn. Make a delivery from floor to table. If the yarn slips, how could you improve the design?

Dinner-Time Delivery:

* Wrap three rubber bands, evenly spaced, around both toilet paper tubes. Slip a pencil through each tube.

* Place 2 chairs on opposite sides of a table, with their backs facing the table. Tie two pieces of yarn to each chair back, then tie the free ends to the pencils, keeping the pencils level to the floor. Wrap the pencil ends loosely with masking tape to keep yarn from sliding.

* Cut and tape paper end to end to create a strip about 4 inches (10 cm) wide and twice the length of the table, plus about 2 ft. (61 cm). Pass the strip over one tube, under the table, up over the other tube, and across the table top. Pull the ends together tightly and tape on both sides.

* Put a toy or small dish on the conveyor belt you've made, and turn one tube so that the paper slides across the table.

Wheels that change an object's direction of motion, or make it easier to lift or move something, are a type of pulley. Your elevator uses one pulley. The conveyor belt is just two pulleys working horizontally. The more pulleys you use vertically, the less force you have to use to lift heavy loads.

> ### Remember to use the Scientific Method!
>
> 1) Make your hypothesis.
> 2) Record your observations.
> 3) Draw your conclusions.

FRACTIONS

Solve the equations using addition.

Hint: Convert to an improper fraction, then find the common denomoninator. The first one has been done for you.

1. $3\frac{1}{3} + 2\frac{1}{6} = \frac{10}{3} + \frac{13}{6} =$

   $\frac{20}{6} + \frac{13}{6} = \frac{33}{6} = 5\frac{3}{6} = 5\frac{1}{2}$

2. $\frac{9}{10} + \frac{1}{2} =$

   _____

3. $\frac{3}{4} + \frac{7}{8} =$

   _____

4. $\frac{8}{9} + \frac{2}{3} =$

   _____

5. $\frac{5}{6} + \frac{11}{12} =$

   _____

6. $\frac{1}{7} + \frac{3}{14} =$

   _____

7. $\frac{4}{6} + \frac{1}{2} =$

   _____

8. $\frac{4}{5} + 2\frac{7}{10} =$

   _____

FRIDAY

Are your knees too shaky for hopscotch?

Use compound words to create path from start to finish.
(Example: ice + box = icebox then, box + car = boxcar)

PIT	FRAME	TOP	HAND	RAIL	WAY	ONE	KIND
SCORE	TRICK	WAGON	OFF	FIRE	OUT	TEAM	OLD
UNDER	FISH	WEIGHT	LIFT	CORK	BACK	WOMAN	HEAD
ONE	POINT	PAPER	LINE	BONE	DOOR	LIKE	RIGHT
CAP	STONE	WALL	CARD	BALL	BELL	HOP	SCOTCH
KNEE	BELT	TEST	GREEN	FOOD	OVER	RAIN	HINGE
AIR	PLAY	LEFT	DOG	CLEAR	LOG	SHIRT	CUB
NAIL	PEEL	LIGHT	CAN	SEAT	TOP	CHEESE	PLAY

START → (KNEE row)

FINISH (SCOTCH)

CROSSWORD

Can you guess the relationship?

Across:

5. Telegram, email, letter

7. Acorn, spaghetti, butternut

9. Qatar, Tajikistan, Bolivia

10. Nutmeg, coriander, saffron

Down:

1. Saphire, ruby, emerald

2. Canine, wisdom, incisor

3. Happy, sad, angry

4. Horse, atomic, solar

6. Christianity, Islam, Judaism

7. Fever, cold, flu

8. Pro-, anti-, mid-

IRREGULAR VERBS

Write the past tense for each verb. Remember, irregular verbs form their past tense by changing their spelling rather than adding "ed."

Example: break → broke

1. do → _____

2. sing → _____

3. bring → _____

4. drive → _____

5. see → _____

6. sleep → _____

7. go → _____

8. swim → _____

Make a Weather Station:
Air in Motion
Adult supervision is recommended.

Materials
fishing line, 108–120 in.
   (274.3–304.8 cm)
dowel or tree branch,
   18 in. (45.7 cm)
scissors
6 discarded compact
   discs or CD-ROMs (can
   also use other items
   such as shells, nails
   or bolts)

Wind is moving air. Differences in air pressure cause air to move. Air moves from areas of high pressure to areas of low pressure.

How do we know when air is moving? We cannot see air in motion, but we can feel it. With a wind chime, you can hear air in motion as it moves objects and knocks them together. Make a wind chime, and listen to how it reacts to moving air.

Directions
1. Cut an 18–20 in. (45.7–50.8 cm) length of fishing line for each disc.

2. Loop a piece of fishing line through the center hole of each disc. Don't tie the line tightly down. Pull the loop through so that the edge of the CD is $\frac{1}{2}$ in. (1.3 cm) or so from the knot. Then tie the other end of the line to the dowel or branch. Space the discs about 2 in. (5.1 cm) apart on the dowel.

3. Tie another piece of fishing line on each end of the dowel or branch to hang the wind chime.

4. Hang your chime in a place where it will be level and will catch a breeze.

Extension

In 1593, Italian scientist and mathematician Galileo invented a thermometer to measure the temperature of the air. His invention marked the beginning of scientific study of the weather. Read about the history of meteorology at your local library. On the lines below, take notes as you research.

_____

_____

_____

_____

_____

_____

_____

_____

_____

_____

_____

YOUR vs. YOU'RE

Circle the correct word for each sentence below.

"Your" shows possession.
"You're" is a contraction for you are.

1. **Your/You're** going to be late.

2. I love **your/you're** bike.

3. Don't forget to tell **your/you're** teacher.

4. I heard **your/you're** going into the 5th grade.

5. **Your/You're** mother said you have to go home.

6. **Your/You're** not going to believe this.

7. I saw **your/you're** brother at the park.

8. **Your/You're** taller than me.

Journal

NOTE: If you need more room, use a blank sheet of paper.

The best television show I watched this week was:

_____

because:_____

_____

_____

_____

DECIMALS

Solve the equations below.
The first one has been done for you.

1.   .9872
      + .1156
      ———
       1.1028

2.   .8296
      − .3611
      ———

3.   .7976
      − .2847
      ———

4.   .5955
      + .5801
      ———

5.   .6696
      − .3988
      ———

6.   .4682
      + .4234
      ———

7.   1.0062
      − .9871
      ———

8.   .1653
      + .2374
      ———

9.   .4291
      + .3768
      ———

Journal

NOTE: If you need more room, use a blank sheet of paper.

TUESDAY

My best friend's name is ______________________________.

I like him/her because... ______________________________

____

____

____

____

____

____

____

____

____

____

MEGA MATH

Find values for each shape and solve the equations.

▲ = ?   ● = 6   ■ = ?

▲ = ● ■

● = ■ ■ ■

$$\frac{▲ \; ● \; ■ \; ■}{■} = ?$$

Ingredients:

oil
pancake batter
milk and eggs
A variety of foods, some that melt, some that don't. Examples: raisins, marshmallows, coconut, chocolate chips, nuts, strawberries, butterscotch chips, etc.

Equipment:

griddle or frying pan
spatula
plates, napkins, forks and bowls

Parental supervision is recommended.

Metamorphic Pancakes!

Directions:

Note: Have an adult help you if you've never made pancakes before. Proceed with making a regular pancake, only create a variety of different batters by adding different foods (of your choice) from the left. As your pancake cooks on the griddle, press down with the spatula creating pressure. Heat and pressure are necessary to form metamorphic rocks!

Finish cooking, eat and enjoy your metamorphic pancakes!

Games Mega-Memory

- Have a box with a variety of different objects, such as pencils, a piece of yarn, a quarter, etc.
- Everyone playing should analyze the box for about 30 seconds.
- After the time is up, cover the box and remove one of the objects.
- Re-position the objects and let everyone have another look at the box.
- The first person who can guess what is missing wins!
- The winner is in charge of the box for the next round.

THE MYSTERY OF THE LOST TIME CAPSULE

Chapter 4

Cody, Klugh and Peyton couldn't speak. Misjiff took off and ran toward the voice.

"Misjiff!" cried Cody. "Come back!"

What Cody saw next made his stomach jump. Misjiff ran straight into a tall, lanky man with long, thin arms. He had a graying ponytail and a scraggly gray beard.

The man raised his arms wide, like the wings of a vulture. "What is this creature?" he growled.

"His name is Misjiff," Cody said, finding his voice. "He's my pet ferret."

The old man glared at Misjiff. Then he reached into the pockets of his sweater.

Peyton gasped, "What's he doing?"

Mr. Warner took two peanuts from his sweater pocket and held them out to the ferret. "I suppose all you want is food," he mumbled. Misjiff took the peanuts and then ran up the steps and into the house.

"No, Misjiff, don't go in there!" Cody yelled.

"Come get your animal," Mr. Warner said. "I don't want any disturbances in my house."

Frightened, Cody, Klugh and Peyton ran inside to rescue Misjiff.

As they searched for the ferret, they noticed that the house was very different from most houses they knew. The floor was uneven and made of thick wooden planks, and the ceiling seemed to begin just above their heads. There was a huge, open fireplace big enough for Cody to stand in. Here Cody found Misjiff, munching his peanuts.

He scooped up his pet and said, "This sure is a cool old house."

"Been in my family as long as I can remember," Mr. Warner muttered. "You kids better go now. I'm not used to having folks around."

Cody, Klugh and Peyton headed for the door. "Thanks for the peanuts," said Cody.

"Chee, chee, chee!" Misjiff chattered.

Mr. Warner dropped another peanut to Misjiff. Cody thought he saw the man begin to smile.

Outside the house, Peyton said, "He's not so scary. I think he's just lonely."

"Did you guys see that house?" asked Klugh.

"His house could be the one," Cody said.

"We should go to the library," said Peyton. "We must do more research."

ACTIVITY 4

Skill: Compound and Complex Sentences

Choose the word that best combines the ideas below. Use each word only once. The first one is done for you.

and   but   because   after   when   so that

1. Cody, Peyton and Klugh are afraid <u>because</u> Misjiff runs up to Mr. Warner.

2. Cody, Peyton and Klugh enter the house _____ Misjiff runs inside.

3. The ceiling of the house was low, _____ the fireplace was huge.

4. Cody thinks he sees Mr. Warner smile _____ Mr. Warner gives Misjiff another peanut.

5. Peyton thinks they should go to the library _____ they can do research.

6. The kids think Mr. Warner will hurt Misjiff, _____ he gives the ferret a peanut.

Question and Answer

Barry Bonds broke the home run record by slugging 73 home runs. The previous record was 70 homers.

Whose record did he break?

FACTOID

Florence Nightingale was a famous nurse in the 1800s. She is best known for her efforts to improve sanitary conditions in hospitals and for her contributions to the training of nurses. Her ideas and principles continue to this day.

Logic Problems

Which comes next?

Can you solve the relationship between the numbers and the words? What would come next?

1	Bee	6	Box
2	Solo	7	Clown
3	Table	8	Coat
4	Door	9	Dive
5	Tire	10	?

Film
Desk
Crayon
Mouse

Weird Science

Solid as a...Mineral?

We wear them, sit on them, write with them, pay with them, and even eat them. "They" are rocks and minerals. All rocks are a mixture of minerals, and some minerals are just one basic element. Check out how they're alike, how they're different, and what some of them are good for.

You will need: egg carton, shoe box, as many rock samples as you can find, magnifying glass, salt, chalk, penny, nail, playdough, plastic knife

Rocks Are Everywhere:

• Go on a mineral scavenger hunt in and around your house. Use your egg carton as a convenient holder for small pieces, and the shoe box for bigger ones.

• Can you find: salt, chalk, talcum powder, a cast iron pan, a pencil, a nickel, a penny, Borax detergent, a piece of marble, a piece of limestone, and quartz?

• Look at the samples with a magnifying glass. Can you see that some look like a mixture of many minerals, while others seem to have just one ingredient?

How Hard Is Hard?

• Try to scratch each rock sample with your fingernail. Does it leave a mark on any of them? If it did, set those aside.

• In a spot where it won't show (you may not be allowed to scratch the marble!), use the penny to scratch the remaining samples. Does that leave a mark? Put those in a pile.

• Do the scratch test a third time with the nail. How do the samples compare at this point? What types of rocks do you think would make strong building blocks? Which ones would last the longest over years of weathering?

Be a Gem Cutter:

• Shape a chunk of playdough into a ball. Flatten the top. Use the plastic knife to slice away eight bits angled from the top as shown, then cut eight long slices angled in toward the bottom. Does your chunk look something like a diamond? Was it easy to make? A true diamond has 58 perfect cuts! Try a cube or a rectangle with slanted edges (a baguette).

Where do rocks play a famous role in the world? Think of Plymouth Rock, the Pyramids, Stonehenge, Mt. Rushmore, the Lincoln Memorial, the Great Wall of China, and the Grand Canyon. Your scratch test is based on the Mohs hardness scale, where talc is rated the softest mineral (a number 1) and diamond is the hardest (number 10). Only a diamond can scratch another diamond. If your fingernail made a scratch, the rating is less than 2 1/2; a penny scratch means less than 3, and a nail is less than 6 1/2.

Certain mineral crystals are valued as gems. You may know blue corundum as sapphire and red corundum as ruby. Look up your birthstone in an encyclopedia.

Remember to use the Scientific Method!

1) Make your hypothesis.

2) Record your observations.

3) Draw your conclusions.

MATH SYMBOLS

Fill in the correct math symbol for each equation below.

1. 64 ☐ 8 = 8

2. 55 ☐ 5 = 11

3. 7 ☐ 7 = 49

4. 882 ☐ 441 = 441

5. 50 ☐ 5 = 250

6. 899 ☐ 11 = 910

7. 99 ☐ 33 = 3

8. 12 ☐ 12 = 144

9. 450 ☐ 16 = 466

FRIDAY

Can you change a shortstop into a manhole?

Use compound words to create path from start to finish.
(Example: ice + box = icebox then, box + car = boxcar)

FINISH

BUNT	STITCH	JERSEY	SENSE	EYES	BASE	HERE	HOLE
OUT	GLASS	PITCH	RAN	GREAT	CALL	CHAIR	MAN
FLY	UMPIRE	TOP	NOTCH	TALL	LEFT	ARM	ERROR
HIT	WALK	PLAY	SECOND	MOUND	STEAL	SIDE	WIND
WIG	BASE	FACE	RING	HAT	HILL	TOP	OUT
GUM	SLAM	DRY	SEAT	SET	UP	FIRST	CAP
RUN	SIGN	UNDER	GLOVE	OFF	CENTER	SEASON	THIRD
SHORT	STOP	LIGHT	WEIGHT	LIFT	SCORE	INNING	LINE

START

55

CROSSWORD

How well do you know analogies?

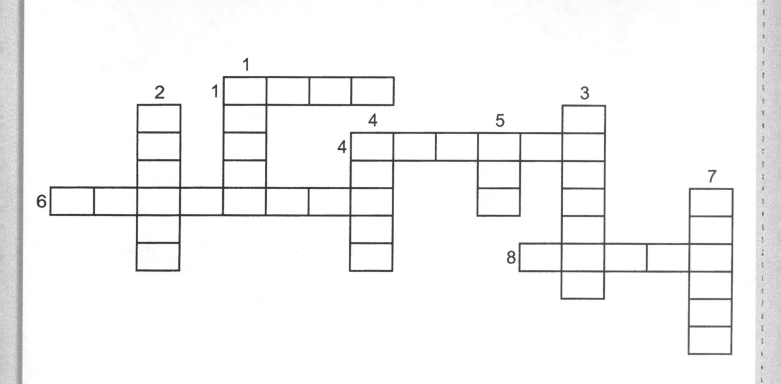

Across:

1. Homerun is to baseball as _____ is to soccer.

4. _____ is to paper as nail is to wood.

6. Positive is to correct as _____ is to wrong.

8. Plane is to fly as car is to _____.

Down:

1. Flour is to flower as grate is to _____.

2. _____ is to eat as tired is to sleep.

3. Numbers are to math as _____ are to spelling.

4. Sugar is to _____ as lemon is to sour.

5. Pizza is to pie as soda is to _____.

7. Heat is to melt as cold is to _____.

THEY'RE, THEIR, THERE

"They're" is a contraction for they are.

"Their" shows possession.

"There" shows direction.

Circle the correct word for each sentence below.

1. **They're/Their/There** is your book.

2. Did you see **they're/their/there** house?

3. I just met **they're/their/there** parents.

4. **They're/Their/There** going to the library.

5. Look over **they're/their/there**!

6. **They're/Their/There** going to have to hurry up!

7. I was **they're/their/there** yesterday.

8. **They're/Their/There** dog was running in the back yard.

Make a Weather Station:
Wind Speed

Adult supervision is recommended.

You have seen that air moves, and you know that it moves at different speeds at different times. Next, you'll make an *anemometer,* or wind gauge. This tool is used to measure wind speed. Cups catch the wind and revolve. The speed of the revolving cups indicates wind speed.

Long before the anemometer was invented, Francis Beaufort of the British Navy created a scale to measure the force of winds at sea. Although this scale helped sailors by giving measure to the force of wind and what happened as a result of this force, Beaufort's scale did not account for the speed of wind. It wasn't until 1926 that the scale was refigured to include measures of speed.

Materials

5 paper cups, 3 oz. (85 g) each
4 straight plastic straws
stapler
hole punch
pencil with an eraser

soft-drink bottle
straight pin
small amount of sand
  or gravel
modeling clay

Directions

1. Punch a single hole about $\frac{1}{2}$ in. (1.3 cm) below the rim in four of the five paper cups. These are the wind cups.

2. In the fifth cup, punch two holes on opposite sides about $\frac{1}{4}$ in. (.6 cm) below the rim. Punch two more holes about $\frac{1}{2}$ in. (1.3 cm) below the rim, also on opposite sides. There should be four holes equally spaced around the cup. Two should be $\frac{1}{4}$ in. (.6 cm) below the rim, and two should be $\frac{1}{2}$ in. (1.3 cm) below the rim. Then punch a hole in the center of the bottom of the cup. This is the center cup.

3. Tape two plastic straws together, end to end. Tape the other two straws the same way. These are spokes.

4. Push one spoke through a hole in one of the wind cups. Pull the straw through the hole. Fold the end of the straw and staple it to the side of the cup opposite the hole.

5. Slide the other end of this spoke through two holes of the center cup so that the straw crosses the middle of the cup.

6. Now add another wind cup on the open end of this spoke. Make sure that this wind cup faces the opposite direction from the first wind cup. Slide the straw through the hole and staple it to the opposite side as you did in step 4.

7. Repeat steps 4 through 6 with the other straws and wind cups.

8. Push a straight pin down through the straws where they cross in the center.

9. Push the eraser end of the pencil up through the bottom of the center cup. Push the straight pin into the eraser.

10. Fill a soft-drink bottle with sand or gravel.

11. Put clay in the bottle opening, and push the pencil into the clay so that it holds the anemometer upright.

12. Place the anemometer where it will catch the breeze. The chart below, based on the Beaufort Scale, shows some ways to estimate wind speed. Use it to estimate and record the wind speed daily in your weather journal.

Wind Speed (mph)	Description
Under 1	Calm. Smoke goes straight up.
1–3	Smoke shows wind direction. Weather vane remains still.
4–7	Feel wind on face; leaves rustle, flags stir.
8–12	Leaves and twigs move in trees. Vanes move.
13–18	Dust blows; small branches move.
19–24	Small trees sway.
25–31	Flags beat in the wind. Wires may whistle.
32–38	Large trees move.
39–46	Walking becomes difficult.
47–54	Some building damage occurs.
55–63	Trees broken; structural damage occurs.
64–73	Serious damage occurs. Trees uprooted.
74+	Hurricane and tornado force; great destruction.

VERBS WORD SEARCH

I	D	F	I	N	I	S	H	E	D	M	B	D	R
J	A	M	T	D	I	T	A	I	B	H	T	C	A
E	N	A	V	I	G	A	T	E	D	E	P	W	J
L	I	E	M	F	S	R	H	A	I	S	Y	A	T
O	T	U	O	P	N	E	A	T	N	I	M	P	E
T	H	I	W	A	B	D	E	I	U	W	T	P	F
U	L	O	E	H	B	S	F	L	R	A	F	E	N
S	M	N	D	P	T	A	H	A	R	S	O	A	S
S	W	H	B	E	G	I	K	T	R	H	B	R	H
M	B	U	S	D	S	G	T	E	H	E	P	E	R
V	N	E	N	K	W	C	H	M	D	S	Q	D	U
A	S	X	I	G	I	Z	Y	G	T	V	I	H	N
B	O	Q	H	V	M	I	C	I	O	N	W	T	O
I	G	L	A	U	G	H	E	D	H	R	I	L	Y

Search for the 10 verbs from the sentences below. The hidden words might be horizontal, vertical or diagonal.

1. Who finished the cereal?   _____
2. I swim in my pool every day.   _____
3. The captain navigated the course.   _____
4. The golfer swung his golf club.   _____
5. My dad mowed the lawn yesterday.   _____
6. We stared at the stars for hours.   _____
7. He appeared to be upset.   _____
8. We laughed at the movie.   _____
9. My mom baked chocolate chip cookies.   _____
10. My neighbor washes his car every Sunday.   _____

60

GRID MAPPING

Map the grid using the ordered pairs below.

The first number locates the horizontal position (across). The second number locates the vertical position (up and down). The first one is done for you.

Example:	(8,6)	
(1, 10)	(7, 6)	(6, 2)
(8, 4)	(2, 8)	(10, 9)
(3, 9)	(4, 7)	(9, 3)

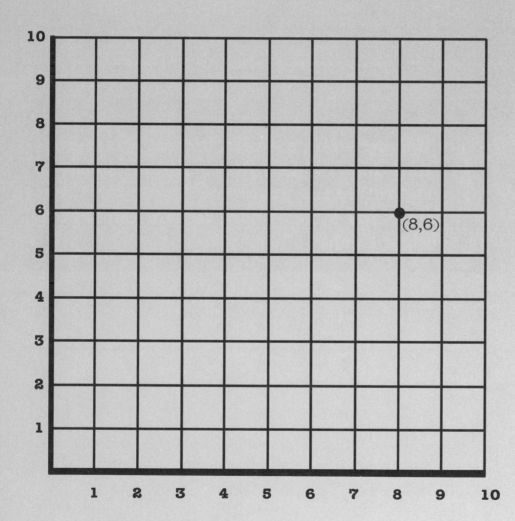

Journal

TUESDAY

Write about something funny that you did when you were little. _____

_____

_____

_____

_____

_____

_____

_____

_____

_____

_____

Use pennies, nickels, dimes, quarters, half dollars, and silver dollars to solve the following problem. You do not have to use each type of coin to solve the riddle. Good Luck!

Lana has a piggy bank. She has $52.40 saved up for a new bike. The money is made up of an equal number of each of four different coins. What coins does she have? How many of each?

Recipes

Parental supervision is recommended.

Tasty Fruit Go-Kart!

Ingredients:
apples
blueberries
strawberries

Equipment:
Popsicle sticks
toothpicks
clear tape
plastic blueberry container

Directions:
First take two Popsicle sticks and tape them together so that they lay flat and are side by side. Next, lay two toothpicks (one on each end) across the bottom side of your Popsicle sticks. Attach the two toothpicks to your Popsicle sticks with tape also. Now take your apples and slice them vertically, about a half-inch (1 cm) space between each slice. (Be careful with the knife!) Stop when you have four separate slices. Stick your apple slices on the ends of your toothpicks and turn your go-kart upside down so that the smooth surface of your Popsicle sticks show. Slide four blueberries on each wheel so that you'll have four hubcaps. Place two or three strawberries in the vehicle (these are your riders!). Cut the blueberry box so it fits and covers your strawberries on top of the vehicle, then attach it with the tape. Now you're ready to roll.

Games   Sounds Around

- All players sit in a circle.
- One designated player begins by making a sound (ex., clapping hands twice).
- The player next to them must clap their hands twice and add another sound of their own.
- Each player adds another sound in addition to the previous sounds they have heard.
- No talking is allowed, although sounds may be made with the mouth.
- If you miss a sound you are eliminated.
- The last one remaining is the winner!

THE MYSTERY OF THE LOST TIME CAPSULE

Chapter 5

Bright and early the next morning, the three friends sat at a table in the research room of the Middletown Public Library.

"We'd better look for that book Ms. Carson read in class," Cody said. "What was it called?"

"*Pioneer Days*," Peyton said.

"I'll find it," Klugh said. "I'm good at finding things." Off he went to the history room, leaving Cody and Peyton to review their plan.

"We need to study that book. If the early settlers' homes had floors and ceilings and fireplaces like Mr. Warner's, we definitely have to go back," Cody said.

"And we have to tell him about the contest," Peyton said. "He's not so scary, Cody. He's just not used to having kids around. I think he'll let us back in."

"Here's the book," Klugh said, plunking it down on the table. They began studying how the pioneers conquered the wilderness.

Paging through the book, Cody, Klugh and Peyton read about the many skills needed by the early settlers, the wild game they ate, the wagons they used to transport their household goods, and the flatboats that carried them across the rivers.

Finally, Cody, Klugh and Peyton found a whole chapter on the pioneer settlement. They read about choosing a place to settle, clearing the land, and building a temporary shelter.

After cutting trees for logs, the settlers had a house-raising. All the men helped carry and place the heavy logs. The women and children filled the spaces between the logs with clay and mud. Earthen floors were eventually covered with thin wooden planks. The large stone hearth served as the kitchen and as a warm gathering place for the family. Cabin ceilings were low, and front doors were thick.

"Listen to this," said Cody. "'Some of the earliest pioneer homes can be found near rivers. Settlers used these rivers to explore new territories.'" Cody stopped reading. "We've got to go back to Mr. Warner's house," he said.

"Will he let us back in?" wondered Peyton.

ACTIVITY 5

Skill: Reading Comprehension—Summarizing

Explain, in order, the steps involved in building a log home.

1. _____
_____

2. _____
_____

3. _____
_____

4. _____
_____
_____

5. _____
_____
_____

FOCUS ON MAIN IDEA

Why is the book *Pioneer Days* helpful to Cody, Peyton and Klugh?

_____
_____
_____
_____

Question and Answer

The cheese used on this food originally came from the milk of the water buffalo.

What food is it?

FACTOID

Galileo Galilei perfected the refracting telescope during the sixteenth century. He was jailed for supporting Copernicus' claim that the earth is not the center of the universe.

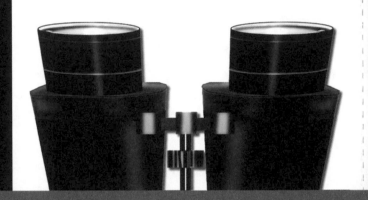

Logic Problems

Which comes next?

Can you solve the relationship between the numbers and the words? What would come next?

1	Onion	6	Sock
2	Tube	7	Sites
3	Think	8	Egg
4	Frog	9	Nylon
5	Foot	10	?

Chair

Text

Base

Dove

Weird Science

Parental Supervision is Recommended.

The Shapes of Nature May Surprise You

You're probably good at drawing circles, squares, triangles and various other shapes, but did you know that Mother Nature does an amazing job, too? It just takes a little hunting...

You will need: a magnifying glass, a small section of lawn, field, beach, forest, etc., several yards (meters) of string or yarn, yardstick (meterstick), a collecting box, camera (optional), sketching paper and pencil

So Easily Missed:

- In your yard, field, beach or woodlands, use the yardstick (meterstick) and string to mark off a square that's about 36 inches (117 cm) on each side.

- Get comfortable on your knees or stomach, and start looking slowly to see the variety of living and non-living occupants of your space. Don't forget to look up, too.

- What things did you find that looked like common shapes? Did you see the spiral pattern in the center of a daisy? The perfectly flat sides of a slice of mica? The pentagon in a starfish? The perfect circles inside toadstools or tree stumps? A hexagon in a bee's honeycomb? You might want to take pictures to start an unusual photo album.

- Go away and come back a few hours later to see what may have changed. Did anyone "move into" your space? Can you now see the oval of a beetle's back, or the symmetry in a butterfly's wings?

One Good Shape Deserves Another:

- If you can, collect some plant life from your square yard (meter) sample. Try to get a complete stem, twig or branch with multiple leaves, clusters, or needles.

- Keeping the leaf grouping intact, sketch its overall shape; is it a stubby or elongated triangle, a long oval, or something else?

- Now look at just one leaf or subgroup of leaves. How does each leaf's shape compare to the complete group's? If there are even smaller groups, look at just one of those leaves with the magnifying glass. What is its shape? Draw it.

- Count the number of sections, needles or leaves at each level of your grouping. Are they the same or multiples of one another?

Did you find repetition and easily recognizable shapes in many of your observations? We may think we create cool patterns when we draw with geometric shapes, but nature really got there first.

Fractals are patterns that, upon magnification, form infinite repeats of the overall pattern. Reproducible with clever math, they appear often in nature (in ferns, clouds, galactic clusters, etc.) and are mesmerizing.

Remember to use the Scientific Method!

1) Make your hypothesis.

2) Record your observations.

3) Draw your conclusions.

EXPANDED NOTATION

Write the following numbers in expanded notation
using place value words and numbers.

Example: 8,662

     Words = 8 thousands + 6 hundreds + 6 tens + 2 ones

     Numbers = 8,000 + 600 + 60 + 2

1. 5,774

Words = ____ thousands + ____ hundreds + ____ tens + ____ ones

Numbers = _____ + _____ + _____ + _____

2. 9,011

Words = ____ thousands + ____ hundreds + ____ tens + ____ ones

Numbers = _____ + _____ + _____ + _____

3. 8,229

Words = ____ thousands + ____ hundreds + ____ tens + ____ ones

Numbers = _____ + _____ + _____ + _____

4. 6,150

Words = ____ thousands + ____ hundreds + ____ tens + ____ ones

Numbers = _____ + _____ + _____ + _____

5. 4,447

Words = ____ thousands + ____ hundreds + ____ tens + ____ ones

Numbers = _____ + _____ + _____ + _____

6. 3,983

Words = ____ thousands + ____ hundreds + ____ tens + ____ ones

Numbers = _____ + _____ + _____ + _____

Can you turn a fruit into an insect?

Use compound words to create path from start to finish.
(Example: ice + box = icebox then, box + car = boxcar)

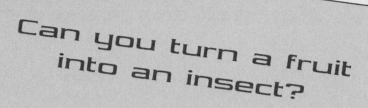

START

HOSE	WATER	PINE	CONE	CAR	PEAR	IN	ORANGE
GRAPE	SOUR	APPLE	SAUCE	HOT	MILK	HOT	PITS
BUG	LEMON	SEED	PAN	FRY	FRENCH	PEEL	BANANA
BACK	RIND	WALK	CAKE	TIN	MAN	SKIN	SIDE
UP	BREAK	OUT	ANGEL	TIME	RACE	HUNT	MOTH
LIFT	LIGHT	BACK	HOUSE	WORK	HORSE	POWER	OUT
OFF	HAND	RAIL	ROAD	OVEN	PLAY	HOUSE	FLY
KIWI	ON	ANT	SIDE	BEE	BITE	BARN	PLANE

FINISH

69

CROSSWORD

How well do you know analogies?

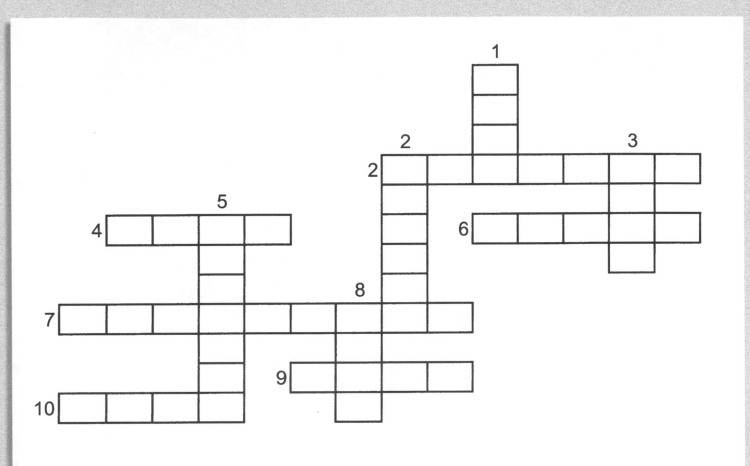

Across:

2. Iowa is to _____ as Alabama is to South.

4. Sad is to jovial as _____ is to difficult.

6. Hearts are to red as clubs are to _____.

7. Seed is to plant as cocoon is to _____.

9. Portugal is to Europe as Mongolia is to _____.

10. Fat is to obese as _____ is to emaciated.

Down:

1. Oak is to _____ as iron is to metal.

2. Alligator is to reptile as panda is to _____.

3. Glove is to hand as _____ is to foot.

5. Three is to nine as four is to _____.

8. School is to _____ as flock is to geese.

ADVERBS

Adverbs tell about verbs.
They answer how and when.

Unscramble the adverbs from the sentences below.

1. "Wait" the boy shouted loudly.   **y u l d l o**

2. I'll finish my chores tomorrow.   **w m o t r o o r**

3. The rain cooled the pavement quickly.   **k y q i c u l**

4. The runner breathed heavily as he ran his last mile.   **a h e v l i y**

5. The politician talked constantly about taxes.   **y s n t o c n a l t**

6. The ballerina leaped gracefully.   **r g a c l u f l e y**

7. The clown juggled clumsily.   **c m l i u s l y**

8. She whispered quietly in church.   **y q i l e t u**

71

Make a Weather Station:
Direction

Adult supervision is recommended.

Direction tells meteorologists where weather comes from and is an important clue for predicting where weather will go. A compass or the sun can be used to give direction.

A compass relies on magnets and the attraction to the Earth's magnetic field. Points on a *compass rose* are used to show direction. *North, south, west* and *east* are known as cardinal directions.

Shadows from the sun give both direction and time. Shadows cast by the sun change direction depending on the time of the day. The location of the shifting shadows is roughly the same each day. Because the location of the shadow remains a constant, we can use their location to mark direction. The sun rises in the east, sets in the west, and points south around noon.

Materials
cardboard
3 craft sticks, each 18 in. (45.7 cm) long
2 stones
shovel
plastic bag
waterproof tape, such as duct tape or electrical tape
scissors
glue

Directions

1. Cut out the compass rose template shown on the next page. You may color or decorate it as you wish. Cut out a circle of cardboard the same size as the template. Then glue the template to the cardboard.

2. Find a place in your yard that will be in the sun all day and that will be close to your weather station. On a sunny morning, push one of the sticks into the ground so that it stands straight up. (You may have to use a shovel to dig a hole that will fit your purposes.)

3. Observe the shadow cast by the stick. Place one of the stones at the end of the shadow to mark the spot.

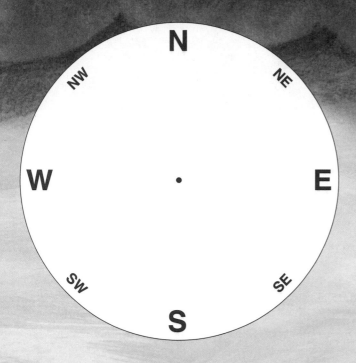

4. Later that afternoon, the shadow will have moved. Place the other marking stone at the end of that shadow.

5. Put your left foot on the "morning" marking stone and your right foot on the "afternoon" marking stone. You are now facing north.

6. Lay one of the other sticks on the ground so that it points just as your nose did when you were facing north. This stick runs north and south.

7. Lay the other stick so that it crosses the first one in a perfect "plus" (+) sign. This stick runs east and west.

8. Put the compass face in the plastic bag. Place it on top of your weather station box so that it faces exactly as your marking sticks on the ground do.

9. Tape the compass into position. Use it to determine what direction the wind is blowing, and record the data in your weather journal.

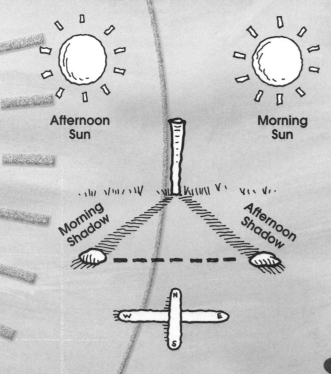

Afternoon Sun

Morning Sun

Morning Shadow

Afternoon Shadow

HELPING VERBS

Circle the helping verbs in each sentence.
Underline the verb phrase (helping verb and main verb).
The first one is done for you.

1. The mechanic (is) fixing the car.

2. We should begin our lesson now.

3. The weather will change tomorrow.

4. The restaurant is serving fish today.

5. They are going shopping later.

6. You might enjoy that television show.

7. The school bus will stop at all railroad crossings.

8. My aunt can play tennis very well.

9. The doctor should explain the procedure to the patient.

10. The river will run faster in the spring.

Journal

NOTE: If you need more room, use a blank sheet of paper.

The last person I talked to on the phone was...

_____

_____

_____

GEOMETRY

Lines, Rays, Line Segments

- A line has no end points. It goes on in both directions.
- A ray is a part of a line. It has one end point and goes on and on in the other direction.
- A line segment has two end points.

Circle line, ray or line segment for each of the following:

1.
    A   P

line   ray   line segment

2.
    B   A

line   ray   line segment

3.
 P   Q

line   ray   line segment

4.
    H   M

line   ray   line segment

5. J   O

line   ray   line segment

6. N   W

line   ray   line segment

Journal

NOTE: If you need more room, use a blank sheet of paper.

If you were given the opportunity to pick where your family would go for a family vacation, where would you choose to go? Why?_____

_____

_____

_____

_____

_____

_____

_____

_____

_____

Use pennies, nickels, dimes, quarters, half dollars, and silver dollars to solve the following problem. You do not have to use each type of coin to solve the riddle. Good Luck!

Danny has $9.66 in loose change in his jacket pocket. If there is an equal number of four different coins, what coins does Danny have? How many of each?

Parental supervision is recommended.

Bisected Finger Dogs

Ingredients:

2 hot dogs
ketchup
mustard
water
hot dog buns

Equipment:

cooking pot
knife

Directions:

Set your hot dogs out on a clean surface. Measure about an inch (3 cm) in from the two ends. Take the knife and cut down the middle of the dog (but not all the way to the bottom!). You should have an incision in the middle of both hot dogs. Boil your dogs as you would regularly. When they are done they should have an open split in the middle but the ends should still be closed. Put them into their buns, and put the ketchup inside the split part of the dog. Put a dab of mustard on one of the ends and spread it around the closed end so that it resembles a fingernail. Eat and enjoy your bisected finger!

Games   Crazy Clarence

- All players sit in a circle.
- One person is in charge.
- The designated person explains that Crazy Clarence has an exclusive club that everyone wants to join.
- However, the only way that people can join is if they figure out what Clarence likes and what he doesn't like.
- The leader can choose what Clarence likes (example: Clarence likes sports that end in the letter 'L', but not sports that end in anything else). Clarence likes baseball, but he doesn't like tennis.
- The leader should have the players randomly guess what Clarence likes and doesn't like; after a while players should catch on.
- No distinct winner, just a lot of fun!

THE MYSTERY OF THE LOST TIME CAPSULE

Chapter 6

Cody, Klugh and Peyton headed down toward the river. They wanted to find out more about the house, but they weren't sure how they'd be received. Misjiff, however, wasn't worried. He ran ahead, eager to see the man who offered him salty peanuts.

"I asked my Mom about Mr. Warner," said Peyton. "She used to play by the river when she was our age. Mom said that Mr. Warner was happy and friendly in those days. He used to show my mom and the other kids different fish and water creatures."

"What happened to him?" Cody asked as they reached the stone wall surrounding Mr. Warner's property. "He sure isn't happy now."

"Mr. Warner was married and his wife died very young. He never got over it. Mom said he was so sad he just kind of shut the door on life," Peyton explained.

"No wonder he was so upset when we all came rushing into his house," Klugh said.

"I feel sorry for him," said Peyton. "He probably doesn't even know how to talk to people after all these years."

Cody gazed at the Warner house. "Everything points to his house being the oldest in town," he said. "Maybe he'd like to hear about the contest and why we think his house could contain the time capsule."

"Chee, chee, chee."

The friends looked up to see Misjiff sitting on Mr. Warner's windowsill. "Chee, chee, chee," he chattered.

The front door opened, and Mr. Warner walked out. "Have you come for more peanuts?" he asked. He reached into his pocket and handed Misjiff two nuts. Then he turned and eyed the three detectives sitting on the old stone wall.

"You're back," he said.

Peyton stepped forward and said, "We have something important to tell you."

"Nobody's had anything to tell me for years," said Mr. Warner glumly. "What could be so important now?"

Cody took a deep breath and asked, "Mind if we come in?"

Mr. Warner seemed to soften. "Do you like cookies?" he asked. Cody saw the shadow of a smile on Mr. Warner's face as he waved them inside.

Skill: Word Recognition—Crossword Fun

Use the clues to find the words in the crossword.

Across:

1. Something that might be buried in the time capsule.

2. Not out.

3. What Cody's pet says.

4. The name of the man who owns the house.

5. Cody has a pet _____.

Down:

1. The name of Cody's pet.

2. Opposite of off.

3. The house is located near a _____.

4. What Cody's pet likes to eat.

5. What we breathe.

Question and Answer

Before there were CDs, before there were even audio cassettes, these were used when people wanted to hear some music. And they aren't records!

Can you name them?

Logic Problems

Which comes next?

Can you solve the relationship between the numbers and the words? What would come next?

1	Ton	6	Fix
2	Glue	7	Heaven
3	Bee	8	Gate
4	Floor	9	Line
5	Drive	10	?

Jar

Pen

Between

Glass

Weird Science

The Floating/Sinking Feeling

Your bar of soap sinks to the bottom of the tub, but a tanker weighing hundreds of thousands of tons floats easily in the ocean—why? Find out with a little morphing magic.

You will need: a sink or dishtub full of water, big cooking spoons made of metal, plastic and wood, bars of different kinds of soap (hand soap, hotel-size, decorative soap, etc.), a solid rubber ball, a hollow ball, empty soda can, a chunk of modeling clay, paper clips, two tall glasses, water, measuring cup and spoons, salt canister and hard-boiled egg

Depends on the Material

• Fill the dishtub about two-thirds full with water. Pick up each soap and decide which seems lightest. Put all the different kinds of soap in the water and see which ones float.

• Weigh the spoons in your hand from lightest to heaviest. Put them in the water. Do any of them float? Put both balls in the water. What happens? What is a hollow ball filled with?

Depends on the Shape

• Does an empty soda can float? Crush it. Does it float?

• Knead the clay into a ball. Drop it into the dishpan of water. Does it float or sink? Squish the clay into roughly a flattened out circle. Drop it into the water. Does it float or sink?

• Reshape the clay again into a boat with a thin hull (try a long canoe shape, a rowboat with one flat end and one pointed bow, or a deep galleon with a plastic straw mast and paper sail). Does it float or sink? What fills it?

• Add paper clips as "cargo," one by one. What happens?

Depends on the Liquid

• Fill the two glasses with one and a half cups of water each. To one glass, add one tablespoon of salt and stir the mixture well. Drop the hard–boiled egg into the plain water glass, and then into the saltwater glass. How does the egg rest in each? Add more tablespoons of salt, one at a time; what happens to the egg after each addition? What if you heat or cool the water first—does it take less or more salt to float?

Two things determine whether an object floats or sinks: the heaviness of an object (mass) divided by its shape (volume). The result of this equation is an object's density. Something very heavy and spread out very wide is not as dense as the water, so it floats. Something lightweight, scrunched into a small shape, is quite dense, and will sink. Some soaps have air whipped into them, which makes them light, while others of the same size are solid and heavy. Is it easier for you to float when you're in a cannonball shape or stretched out on your back? In deep water or shallow water?

Do you know that a gallon (4 liters) of plain water weighs about eight pounds (4 kg)? As long as something weighs less than the volume of water it pushes aside, and at least that amount of water weight remains, that something will float. Estimate how many gallons (liters) of water it would take to float yourself. Then, find out what's unique about swimming in the Dead Sea (located between Israel and Jordan in the Middle East).

Remember to use the Scientific Method!

1) Make your hypothesis.

2) Record your observations.

3) Draw your conclusions.

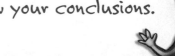

NUMBER SEARCH

Write out the number for each and then circle each number in the Number Search. Numbers may run up, down or diagonally.

1. five million six hundred sixty-seven thousand eleven _____

2. three hundred sixty-nine thousand three hundred thirty-nine _____

3. eighty-six million six hundred twenty-four thousand eight hundred fifty-three _____

4. six hundred seventy-two thousand seven hundred fifty-six _____

5. nine hundred twenty-six thousand eight hundred forty-four _____

6. one million two hundred eighteen thousand five hundred seventy-six _____

7. thirty-one million eight hundred twenty-five thousand seven hundred fifty-five _____

8. three million six hundred and one thousand five hundred fifteen _____

9. fourteen million two hundred eighty thousand fourteen _____

10. sixty-two million four hundred seventy-seven thousand four hundred three _____

5	6	2	4	7	7	4	0	3	0
8	3	1	8	2	5	7	5	5	8
6	9	1	2	1	8	5	7	6	4
6	2	6	7	2	7	5	6	1	1
2	6	2	3	9	1	7	0	1	9
4	8	0	4	5	5	0	0	3	7
8	4	6	1	8	8	7	3	9	3
5	4	0	1	2	6	9	2	1	4
3	6	2	4	6	6	8	5	2	9
3	1	1	5	3	2	5	8	1	3

You're the cat.
Find your house!

**Use compound words to create path
from start to finish.
(Example: ice + box = icebox then,
box + car = boxcar)**

TEA	SPOON	LABOR	MAN	UP	IN	HOME	SICK
CUP	BOWL	STRIKE	WORM	FRONT	BOAT	CHILD	SEA
CAT	FISH	NET	BOOK	STORE	HOUSE	WIFE	THREE
LONG	TAIL	BACK	HAND	ROOM	TOP	SOIL	BLIND
BLUE	FIN	STAGE	POLISH	SADDLE	SIDE	LINE	MICE
TREE	HOLD	HOUSE	LUNCH	BAG	SPIN	STEP	FATHER
FIELD	OUT	BOAT	LINE	PIPE	SMOKE	SON	SET
HOUSE	TRAP	POWER	MAN	KIND	BACK	HOME	WORK

START

FINISH

CROSSWORD

How well do you know your vocabulary?

Hint: An **antonym** is a word that means the opposite of another word. A **homonym** is a word that has the same sound and often the same spelling but different meaning as another word.

Across:

2. Antonym for gentle.
4. Homonym for sun.
5. Antonym for flawed.
6. Synonym for exhibit.
8. Homonym for two.

Down:

1. Antonym for fake.
3. Synonym for jubilant.
4. Synonym for stern.
5. Synonym for courteous.
7. Homonym for poor.

84

VOCABULARY QUIZ

Circle the word that matches the definition.

Hint: An **antonym** is a word that means the opposite of another word.
A **homonym** is a word that has the same sound and often same spelling, but different meaning as another word.

1. **complement**   praise, admiring comment
   compliment

2. **confident**   close, trustworthy person
   confidant

3. **desert**   dish served at the end of a meal,
   dessert   usually sweet

4. **fair**   entrance fee
   fare

5. **hoarse**   gruff, gravelly in sound
   horse

Make a Weather Station:
Make a Wind Vane
Adult supervision is recommended.

One of the oldest tools for checking wind direction is the *wind vane.* You can use it to tell which direction the wind is coming from and watch as the wind changes direction. The wind blows on the vane, which turns until it moves aside from the wind's pressure. The arrow points to the direction from which the wind is coming. If the arrow is pointing to *N,* the wind is blowing from the north—the arrow will be pointing into the wind.

Some people get confused because a north wind blows southward. Just remember that the arrow points to the direction from which the wind is coming. If the arrow points to *W,* the wind is coming from the west, not going there.

Winds are named according to the direction that they blow. This air movement is important to weather forecasting in the northern hemisphere. Winds blowing from the northwest are typically drier and colder. Easterly winds bring clouds and precipitation. Warm, humid weather is brought in by southerly winds.

Materials
soft-drink bottle
$8 \frac{1}{2}$ in. × 11 in.
   (21.6 cm × 27.9 cm) paper
modeling clay
sand or gravel for weight
straight pin
plastic straw

marker
2 plastic coffee can lids
   (or similar soft plastic lids)
ruler
scissors
tape
pencil with eraser

Directions
1. Trace the patterns on the next page onto a sheet of paper. Cut out the tracings, and then use them to trace the patterns onto the plastic lids.

2. Carefully cut out the shapes on the plastic lids.

3. Insert the tabs into each end of the plastic straw. You may have to curl the tabs slightly to get them in securely. Tape the tabs in place.

4. Measure the straw so that you know exactly where its middle is.

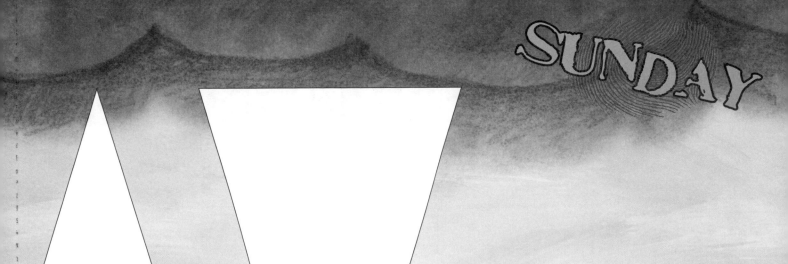

5. Push a pin through the exact middle of the soda straw and into the pencil eraser.

6. Put sand or gravel in the soft-drink bottle.

7. Place some modeling clay in the opening of the bottle. Then place the pencil in the clay so that the pencil stands upright.

8. Mark *N*, *E*, *W* and *S* at equal distances around the bottle.

9. Place the wind vane on top of the weather station along with your compass. Adjust the bottle so that the *N* on the bottle matches the position of the *N* on the compass.

10. Observe the direction of the wind and record your observations daily in your weather journal.

MATH CROSSWORD

**Try to solve this puzzle using your math skills!
The example is bolded to help you get started!**

Across:

1. Two tens
4. Digits add to 19
7. One-third of 90
8. Eight squared
9. Digits add to 25
11. Half of 18 across
13. One better than James Bond
15. 18 across minus 17 down
18. 3 down times 22 down
19. (1 down times 4 down) minus three
23. (Five times 1 down) minus 3
24. 4 x (25 down minus 6 down)
26. Perfect vision
27. Its digits add to 24

Down:

1. Its digits add to 6
2. 4 down + 15 across +1
3. James Bond
4. three times 11 across
5. 7 across x 17 down
6. 17 down - 1 down
10. 1/3 of 23 across
12. Sum of 11 across and 15 across
14. 11 across minus 20 down
16. Last two digits - first two digits = 21
17. Square of last digit in 3 down
18. 8 across times 22 down
20. Its digits add to 4
21. 1 down times 3 down
22. One more than 9 squared
25. 15 across divided by 15

FRACTION PUZZLE

Add diagonally to solve for A, B, C and D.
Then, add A, B, C and D together to solve
for E.

A_____ + B_____ + C_____ + D_____ = E_____

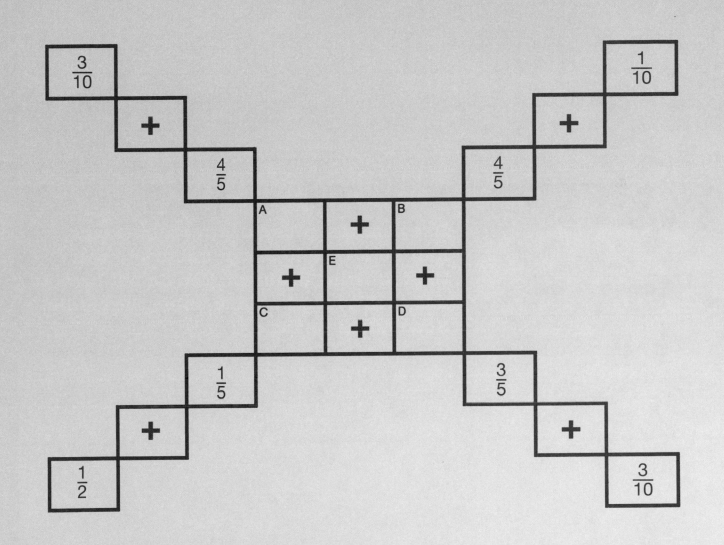

Journal

NOTE: If you need more room, use a blank sheet of paper.

TUESDAY

Finish this story: I thought the summer would be boring, but I changed my mind on the first morning of summer vacation. I rode my skateboard over to the fort my friends and I had built last year and I was amazed when I saw...

_____

_____

_____

_____

_____

_____

_____

_____

_____

_____

MEGA MATH

Use pennies, nickels, dimes, quarters, half dollars, and silver dollars to solve the following problem. You do not have to use each type of coin to solve the riddle. Good Luck!

Leslie and Shannon are running a car wash to earn extra money. They have collected exactly $38 so far. If they have an equal number of five different coins, what coins do they have? How many of each?

Recipes

Parental supervision is recommended.

Chewy Moth Balls

Ingredients:

hard-shell gumballs
5-10 oz (140-280 g)
white chocolate
powdered sugar

Equipment:

saucepan
pair of tongs or a spoon
bowl
wax paper

Directions:

Put the white chocolate in the saucepan and heat over a low to medium flame. Put your gumballs in the bowl. Once chocolate has melted down to a pourable liquid, carefully pour it over your gumballs, making sure to coat them well. Let the mothballs cool for about 5 minutes, then spread powdered sugar on your wax paper and roll the mothballs gently over the sugar to coat them. Let them cool for 10 more minutes. Enjoy!

Games   Attention Please!

- This game works best with a large group of people.
- The two oldest in the group are picked to come before the audience.
- The audience huddles and decides on a topic. They then inform the two in front of that topic.
- The two people must talk about the chosen topic for 30 seconds in front of the audience, but they must do it at the same time. The two speakers can do whatever they want to hold attention, but they must talk about the topic at all times.
- After 30 seconds have expired, the audience must vote on which person held their attention for the most amount of time.
- Pick two new people to be speakers now.

THE MYSTERY OF THE LOST TIME CAPSULE

Chapter 7

Cody, Peyton and Klugh sat with Mr. Warner at the kitchen table, eating chocolate chip cookies.

"These are as good as my mom's," said Klugh.

"I don't have much to do these days," said Mr. Warner, "so sometimes I bake cookies."

Misjiff jumped up on Mr. Warner's lap. "Chee? Chee?" he asked.

"Misjiff!" Cody said. "Don't bother Mr. Warner."

Mr. Warner handed Misjiff two more peanuts and said, "He's no bother." The old man leaned back in the chair and Misjiff climbed to his shoulder, crunching on the peanuts. "I like animals."

"Mr. Warner," Klugh began, "this week Middletown is celebrating its bicentennial. That means the town is 200 years old."

"So? What's got you kids so interested in me and my old house?" Mr. Warner asked.

"There's a contest," said Peyton. "It's to find a time capsule buried during the centennial celebration 100 years ago."

"The time capsule was buried in the town's oldest building," Cody explained. "We think your house could be it."

Mr. Warner frowned. "Why would you think that?"

Cody, Klugh and Peyton began explaining all the clues that had led them to Mr. Warner's house. They told him about its location on the river and the old stone wall marking the property line. They explained how they noticed the large cooking hearth, the low ceiling, and the wooden planks of the flooring.

"Well, I know the house is very old, but I don't know how old, and I certainly don't know anything about a time capsule," said Mr. Warner. "All I have is a box of old family stuff. It's been here as long as I can remember."

"What kind of old stuff?" the detectives asked all at once, unable to contain their excitement.

The old man rubbed his hands along his chin thoughtfully. "Well, let's see, there are some old newspapers and coins, some Indian artifacts, and—"

"Wow!" cried Cody. "Can we see the box?"

WEDNESDAY

Skill: Critical Reading—
Character Analysis

Readers get to know characters by what the characters say and do. Choose a word to describe the characters named below. Give examples of what these characters say and do to reveal their individual traits.

Cody

_____

_____

Klugh

_____

_____

Peyton

_____

_____

_____

Misjiff

_____

_____

_____

Mr. Warner

_____

_____

Question and Answer

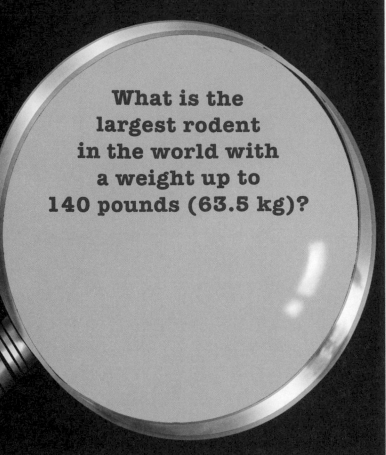

What is the largest rodent in the world with a weight up to 140 pounds (63.5 kg)?

FACTOID

Polaris, also called the North Star, always marks due north. All other stars shift their positions during the night.

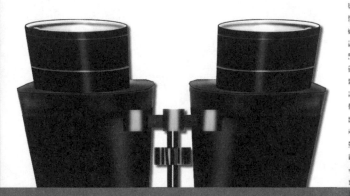

grid LOGIC

Four friends each own a different pet. Based on the clues below, can you figure out each child's first and last name and the type of pet each owns?

	Emily	Abigail	Tyrone	Matthew	Cat	Dog	Snake	Rabbit
Miller								
Su								
Baker								
Evans								
Cat								
Dog								
Snake								
Rabbit								

For examples and instructions on how to complete Grid Logic, turn to the back of the book.

1. One of the girls has a last name that begins with the same letter as the type of pet she owns.
2. Tyrone is going to buy a bone for his canine and the Evans girl is going to get a brush.
3. Matthew and the Miller child are afraid of Emily's reptile.
4. Neither of the boys own a cat because they are both allergic.

Weird Science

Bending, Bouncing Light

By the time sunlight bounces off something and into your eyes (you "see" it), it's really gone through a lot—the atmosphere, some clouds, a little dirt, and maybe even a window. You can make it do more tricks, and find out it still obeys some very strict rules.

You will need: 1 clear glass, straws, water, honey, vegetable oil, corn syrup, pan or plastic container, flat mirror (okay to get wet), white paper, scissors, table in the sunshine, lamp, Playdough, books, pencil and ruler

The Unbroken Broken Straw:

• Fill a clear glass halfway with water. Hold a straw behind the glass and look through at the water's edge. What do you see? Does moving your head change the view?

• Hold straws behind clear bottles of vegetable oil, honey and corn syrup and view from different angles. Do the straws look the same as the straw behind the water?

When White is Full of Color:

• Put the pan/container on the sunny table. Fill it 2 inches (5 cm) deep with water (be careful emptying it later). Hold a piece of white paper standing up along one outside edge.

• With your other hand, hold the mirror in the water, opposite the paper, leaning it at an angle until sunlight falls directly on it and reflects toward the paper. You've created a prism! What does the light on the paper look like? Try again using a shadeless lamp near the table as the light source. Now what's on the paper?

How Far is a Reflection?

• Prop a small mirror straight up against books, in the middle of a flat piece of white paper/cardboard. Cut 2 straws in half. Stick one in a small blob of playdough on the paper, 3 inches (8 cm) in front of the mirror. Stick the other straw in a second blob.

• Looking in the mirror, line up the second straw with the reflection of the first one. Draw a line on the paper between the two. Move the second straw around and draw more lines from it to the reflection of the first straw.

• Remove the books and mirror. With a ruler, continue the lines across the paper. Where do they mostly meet?

Sunlight is really a combination of different wavelengths of colored light; lamplight shows as only one color passing through the white, frosted bulb. Different wavelengths bend different amounts in the different thicknesses of the water wedge prism—red bends, or refracts, the least and violet refracts the most. Water of a constant thickness bends all the light from the straw at once, but oil, honey and corn syrup refract it differently. Reflection makes an image appear behind a mirror the same distance as the object in front.

Put a small rock or leaf in a glass. Wrap plastic wrap over the top, and put a large drop of water on it. The rounded water will bend the light that reflects from the rock, acting as a lens or magnifying glass.

Remember to use the Scientific Method!

1) Make your hypothesis.

2) Record your observations.

3) Draw your conclusions.

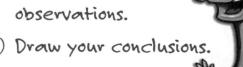

ADJECTIVE OR NOUN?

Sometimes a noun can also be an adjective. Circle whether the bold word in each sentence is being used as a noun or an adjective.

Example: Carrots are my favorite **vegetable**. (noun) adjective

Do you have a **vegetable** garden? noun (adjective)

1. I want to learn to play **tennis**. noun adjective

2. Are you a **tennis** player? noun adjective

3. My grandmother gave me a **picture** frame. noun adjective

4. Who painted that **picture**? noun adjective

5. I love to drink **apple** juice. noun adjective

6. My favorite kind of **apple** is Macintosh. noun adjective

7. I am allergic to **chocolate**. noun adjective

8. That **chocolate** ice cream is rich. noun adjective

9. I like to watch **football**. on television noun adjective

10. Do you have a favorite **football** team? noun adjective

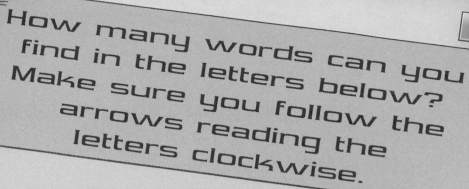

How many words can you find in the letters below? Make sure you follow the arrows reading the letters clockwise.

(Hint: Words may be hidden inside other words.) Use the center space to write the words you find. 30 is good, 40 is great, and 54 is outstanding!

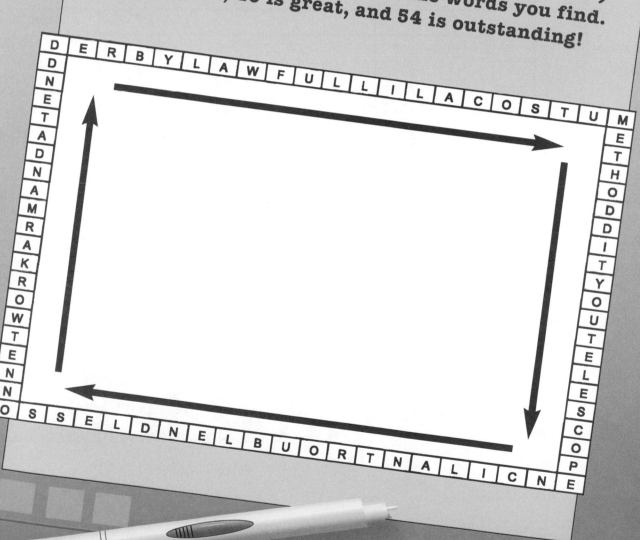

CROSSWORD

Can you guess the relationship?

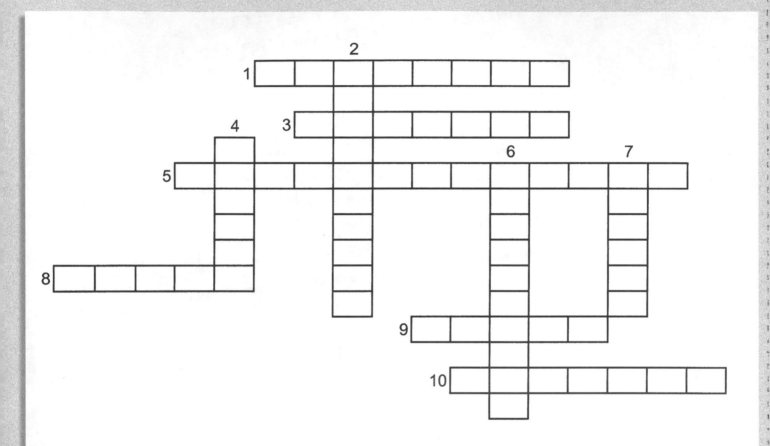

Across:
1. Iguana, rattlesnake, caiman
3. Necklace, bracelet, earring
5. Rain, hail, snow
8. Pliers, saw, wrench
9. Femur, ulna, humerus
10. Liter, centimeter, milligram

Down:
2. Adams, Lincoln, Roosevelt
4. Rye, wheat, pumpernickel
6. Refrigerator, toaster, microwave
7. Stomach, heart, kidney

FACT VS. OPINION

A **fact** is something that can be proved. An **opinion** is what someone thinks or feels about something.

Circle whether each sentence is a fact or an opinion.

1. Summer is the best season of the year.   **fact**   **opinion**

2. Dinosaurs are extinct.   **fact**   **opinion**

3. Canada, Mexico and the United States are located in North America.   **fact**   **opinion**

4. The music is too loud.   **fact**   **opinion**

5. Football is better than baseball.   **fact**   **opinion**

6. The movie ticket costs $5.00.   **fact**   **opinion**

7. Insects are creepy.   **fact**   **opinion**

8. The freezing point is 32 degrees Fahrenheit and 0 degrees Celsius.   **fact**   **opinion**

Make a Weather Station:
Measure Temperature
Adult supervision is recommended.

Temperature is measured in degrees. You may not realize it, but there is more than one scale for measuring temperature. The scale most often used in the United States is called the Fahrenheit system. On this scale, water freezes at 32 degrees (32°F) and boils at 212 degrees (212°F). This is the scale that an American weather forecaster usually reports.

Most people around the world use another scale. This scale, called the Celsius scale, is based on the metric system. In the Celsius scale, water freezes at 0 degrees (0°C) and boils at 100 degrees (100°C).

Another scale, the Kelvin scale, establishes a point of *absolute zero,* or the point at which molecules have the lowest energy. Unlike the other scales, temperature in the Kelvin scale is not measured in degrees, but in Kelvin (K). This scale is closely related to the Celsius scale. The difference in freezing and boiling points of water in both the Celsius and Kelvin scales is 100 degrees, giving both scales the same magnitude. The Kelvin scale is used as the international standard when working with scientific temperature measurements. This is because scientific formulas are more easily expressed when starting at absolute zero.

Materials
inexpensive thermometer
weather station box

waterproof tape, such as duct tape or electrical tape

Directions
1. Tape a thermometer to the backside of the weather station box. Remember, the *backside* of the box will be opposite the box opening.

2. Record temperatures, daily, in your weather journal in both the Fahrenheit and Celsius systems. If your thermometer has just one scale, use the chart on the next page to determine the other scale reading.

3. At the end of each week, graph your results.

Fahrenheit to Celsius Conversion Chart

Fahrenheit	Celsius
-25	-31.7
-20	-28.9
-15	-26.1
-10	-23.3
-5	-20.6
0	-17.8
5	-15
10	-12.2
15	-9.4
20	-6.7
25	-3.9
30	-1.1
35	1.7
40	4.4
45	7.2
50	10
55	12.8
60	15.6
65	18.3
70	21.1
75	23.9
80	26.7
85	29.4
90	32.2
95	35
100	37.8
105	40.6
110	43.3

To convert Fahrenheit to Celsius: Subtract 32 from the Fahrenheit temperature, and then multiply by $\frac{5}{9}$.

To convert Celsius to Fahrenheit: Multiply the Celsius temperature by $\frac{9}{5}$, and then add 32.

Extension

Practice converting temperatures by completing the chart below. Use the formulas listed above to find the equivalent temperatures.

Fahrenheit	Celsius
-31	
	-11
	1
53	
78	
	30
101	

MATH CROSSWORD

Try to solve this puzzle using your math skills!
The example is bolded to help you get started!

Across:

1. Five more than half of 20 down
3. 5 down reversed
5. Two times 13 across
7. Five less than 22 across
9. Three times 20 down
10. One less than twice 18 down
11. 14 down minus 9 across
13. Sixteen times 20 down
15. 7 down minus 13 across
17. 5 down squared
19. 5 across minus one more than 1 down
22. 8 down times 17 across
25. The difference between its digits is two
26. One more than twice 5 down

Down:

1. 4 down plus ten
2. 23 down plus 4 down
3. Two more than five times 5 down
4. Five less than (20 down minus 8 down)
5. One less than 20
6. Nine more than 25 across times three
7. The sum of 13 across and 15 across
8. Eight more than 5 down
10. 8 down plus one hundred
12. 14 down plus 17 across
14. Seven times 3 across
15. Its digits add to 12
16. 9 across minus 10 down
18. The product of 3 times 5 down
20. 5 down plus 8 down
21. Two times 1 down
23. 3 down minus 1 down
24. Seven squared

DECIMAL PUZZLE

Use a calculator to add the numbers together. Start at the bottom, adding side by side. Your answer goes in the row above. Keep adding until you have solved the puzzle.

8.5									
1.7	6.8	.3	2.2	5.6	.14	.98	.02	.74	6.9

Journal

NOTE: If you need more room, use a blank sheet of paper.

TUESDAY

Write about a time that you had to do something that was really hard for you. _____

_____

_____

_____

_____

_____

_____

_____

_____

_____

MEGA MATH

Use pennies, nickels, dimes, quarters, half dollars, and silver dollars to solve the following problem. You do not have to use each type of coin to solve the riddle. Good Luck!

Art used a metal detector to find change on the beach. He found $8.19. If his recovered treasure is made up of an equal number of five different coins, what coins did he find? How many of each?

Recipes

Parental supervision is recommended.

Gooey Fries

Ingredients
2 small potatoes
honey
cooking oil

Equipment
small dipping bowl
frying pan

Directions:
Peel your potatoes so that there is no skin left on. Carefully slice them into long, neat strips. Put enough cooking oil in the pan to cover the bottom and heat on medium to high. Put your potato strips (fries) in the pan and cook until golden brown (or however you like them). Fill a small dipping bowl about an inch and a half (4 cm) high with honey. Let your fries cool for about 10 minutes after they've cooked. Dip your fries in the honey and enjoy!

Games   As the Dog Chases Its Tail

- You will need at least 5 players to play.

- Everyone stands in a line with their hands on the shoulders of the person in front of them.

- The person in front of the line is the head of the dog, the one in back is the tail.

- The line remains straight until the signal is given.

- Someone in the group says, "Look at that dog chase its tail."

- When that signal is given the head runs around toward the tail and tries to touch it. However, the whole body must move with the head without breaking apart.

- If the head touches the tail, the head remains and the tail is changed.

- If the body breaks before the head can touch the tail, the head becomes the tail and everyone moves up one space.

THE MYSTERY OF THE LOST TIME CAPSULE

Chapter 8

Mr. Warner rose from his chair and moved to the side of the stone hearth. Reaching up, he pulled a small wooden box from an opening cut into the wall.

He placed the box on the table and sat down. The wooden box was dusty, but Mr. Warner carefully wiped it clean, revealing a shiny oak finish. The hinges were brass, and so was the clasp that latched the box shut.

Klugh picked up the box and began inspecting it, running his fingers along the opening. "Do you think it used to be sealed, Mr. Warner?" he asked. "This feels like wax."

"Yes, it did have a seal at one time," the old man replied.

When Mr. Warner lifted the lid, the three friends were surprised to see that it was lined with a heavy metal.

"Keepsake boxes were lined in lead in the old days to keep their contents safe from fire and water damage," Mr. Warner explained.

"Cool," said Cody.

"What's this?" asked Klugh, holding up a small, flat square case.

Mr. Warner took the case and opened it carefully. Inside was a faded photograph of a family standing in front of a pioneer home.

"This is a daguerreotype," Mr. Warner said. "It's a very early form of photography."

Klugh studied the daguerreotype and asked, "Mr. Warner, can we take this outside? We need to do a little detective work."

"Just be very careful with it," Mr. Warner said. "It can't be replaced."

Cody, Peyton and Klugh went into the yard and stood on the sidewalk, first staring at the photograph and then back at the house. Together they matched up the stone wall around the house, the stone path leading to the front door, and the small tree, now a giant oak.

"Look at the man in the picture," Peyton said. "He looks like you, Mr. Warner."

"Why, that's my great-grandfather, Josiah B. Warner," Mr. Warner said, flipping the picture over. Written neatly in old-fashioned script was the date, July 1848.

"Looks like we've got more research to do," Cody said. "We need to check these names and dates with the town records."

"We'll be back, Mr. Warner," Peyton said as the children ran off toward the town hall.

ACTIVITY B

Skill: Adjectives—Word Search

Adjectives are words that describe things. They tell which one, what kind, and how many. Find the adjectives in the word search below. All the adjectives were used in Chapter 8.

B	C	S	T	B	G	E	W
Q	U	T	M	R	I	W	O
O	F	O	S	A	F	E	O
A	H	N	P	S	E	L	D
K	E	E	P	S	A	K	E
D	A	G	O	H	R	I	N
K	V	O	L	I	L	U	C
B	Y	R	D	N	Y	I	P
D	U	S	T	Y	F	C	D

brass	old
dusty	safe
early	shiny
heavy	stone
keepsake	wooden
oak	

Question and Answer

Who is the musical artist that has the best selling album of all time?

FACTOID

The Great Wall of China is more than 3,600 miles (5,792 km) long and can be seen from outer space! It was built to protect the country from invading Mongol tribes.

grid LOGIC

Amir and his three friends each bought a computer program. Based on the clues below, can you figure out each child's first and last name and the name of the program they bought?

	Alison	Cecily	Amir	Dominick	Super Reader	Space Voyager	Math Master	Adventure!
Parker								
Bucetti								
Alexander								
DuBois								
Super Reader								
Space Voyager								
Math Master								
Adventure!								

For examples and instructions on how to complete Grid Logic, turn to the back of the book.

1. Both Cecily and the Bucetti child bought educational software.

2. The Alexander boy and Dominick both live near the child who bought "Adventure!"

3. Dominick and the child who bought "Math Master" ride the bus with the Parker child.

108

Weird Science

Parental supervision is recommended.

The Long and Short of Musical Tones

You may think of musical notes as high or low but they really come in long or short—wavelengths, that is. Sound waves travel through the atmosphere by vibrating air molecules; we measure these vibrations by how fast they happen (their frequency). Make some waves yourself.

You will need: 8 drinking glasses or glass jars roughly the same size, water, measuring cup (1 cup = 8 oz or 240 ml), metal spoon, a shallow box or a shoebox lid, rubber bands of different widths, single-strand thin wire or strong button thread, a board 6 in. (15 cm) wide by 2 ft. (60 cm) long, hammer, thin nails, and tape measure

Drinking Glass Bells:

- Line up the 8 glasses on a counter. Fill #1 (on the left) with 8 oz (240 ml) of water. Fill #8 (on the right) with 4 oz (120 ml).

- As best you can, fill the remaining glasses as follows: #2 (7.5 oz/220 ml), #3 (6.75 oz/200 ml), #4 (6.25 oz/185 ml), #5 (5.75 oz/170 ml), #6 (5.125 oz/150 ml), and #7 (4.5 oz/130 ml).

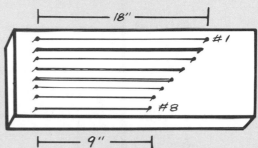

- Tap along the row with a spoon and listen for increasing or decreasing tones. "Tune" them by taking out, or pouring in, tiny amounts of water. Play a "scale."

Box Guitar:

- With the open side of the box, or box lid facing up, slide three or more rubber bands of different widths onto the box widthwise. Strum them with your finger to make sounds.

- Change the order of the rubber bands to go from low to high tones.

Tuning Up Some Strings:

- Draw a line across one end of the board, about 2 inches (5 cm) in from the edge. Mark off 8 dots evenly spaced along this line. With adult supervision, hammer nails halfway in at each dot.

- Measure 18 in. (46 cm) from the first dot, and mark dot #1. Hammer a nail in there. Measure 9 in. (23 cm) from the last dot, and hammer a nail at dot #8. At the following distances, add dots and nails: #2 (16"/41 cm), #3 (14.25"/36 cm), #4 (12.625"/32 cm), #5 (12"/30 cm), #6 (10.75"/27 cm), and #7 (9.5"/24 cm).

- Wrap wires, thread and rubber bands from one nail to another, and pluck them. Tune by pulling tightly. It's not easy!

There are exact mathematical correlations between tones (frequencies). High C on a piano (which works by "hammers" hitting different length wires) comes from hitting a wire that is half the length of the wire that gives middle C (and the high C wire vibrates twice as fast). The note G comes from hitting a wire that is two-thirds the length of the middle C wire; it vibrates 1.5 times as fast. Your water glass #1 holds half the amount of water as #8, but differences in the glasses themselves make the tones differ greatly.

Music or math books can tell you exactly how the string lengths are calculated. Middle C vibrates at 261 times/sec (hertz or Hz) and high C at 523 Hz. Other tones are special multiples of those frequencies.

> ### Remember to use the Scientific Method!
>
> 1) Make your hypothesis.
> 2) Record your observations.
> 3) Draw your conclusions.

MAKE A BAR GRAPH

Make a bar graph using the monthly sales figures from Company X. January has been completed for you.

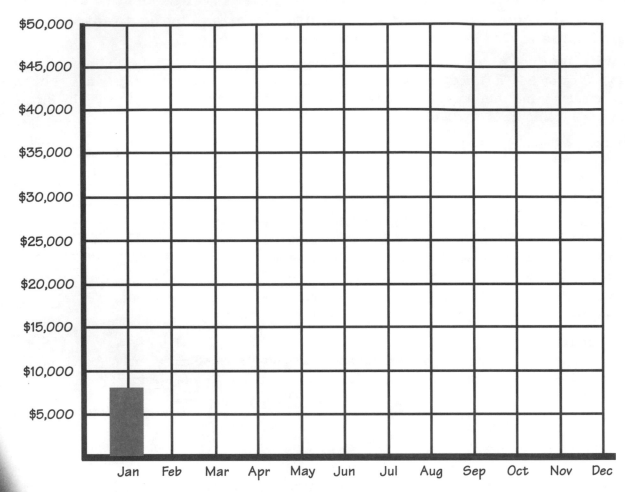

Company X Monthly Sales

Month	Sales Dollars
January	$8,500
February	$12,000
March	$20,000
April	$18,000
May	$24,000
June	$28,000
July	$27,000
August	$24,000
September	$29,000
October	$36,000
November	$42,000
December	$49,000

How many words can you find in the letters below? Make sure you follow the arrows reading the letters clockwise.

(Hint: Words may be hidden inside other words.)
Use the center space to write the words you find.
28 is good, 32 is great, and 38 is outstanding!

CROSSWORD

Can you guess the relationship?

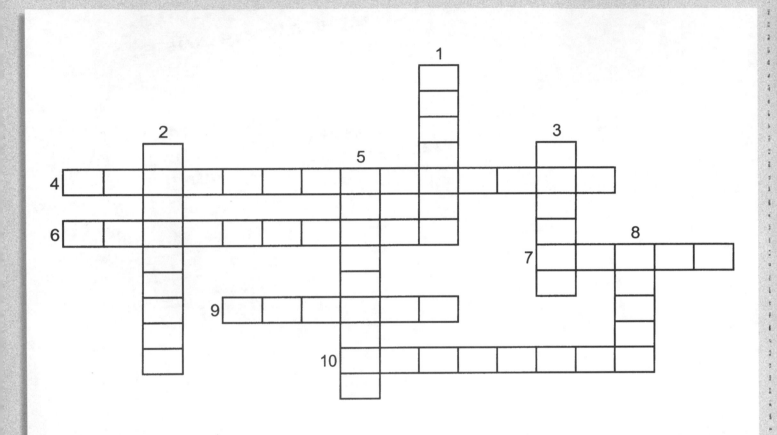

Across:

4. Bus, ferry, subway

6. Onion, broccoli, carrot

7. Igneous, sedimentary, metamorphic

9. Banana, melon, orange

10. Iron, potassium, helium

Down:

1. Whale, horse, porcupine

2. English, Spanish, German

3. Ecru, magenta, teal

5. Uncle, niece, grandmother

8. Penny, nickel, dime

ABBREVIATIONS

Search for the 10 words represented by the abbreviation listed below. The hidden words might be horizontal, vertical or diagonal.

R.N.

Dr.

Mr.

TV

St.

Ave.

VIP

C.O.D.

Rd.

Blvd.

O	M	W	A	B	F	M	N	D	I	P	J	L	O	K	E	H
I	O	M	S	Q	X	T	E	R	E	T	N	G	I	N	S	V
N	C	O	E	N	A	R	O	E	S	E	I	D	L	R	W	E
Z	T	A	L	I	M	W	T	G	D	L	U	C	L	K	O	R
B	A	I	S	T	C	V	Y	I	O	E	U	K	B	R	O	Y
D	E	F	J	H	A	B	U	S	N	V	C	A	E	I	L	I
A	R	J	A	D	O	I	H	T	B	I	R	T	D	F	L	M
I	P	N	L	D	A	N	I	E	X	S	S	N	O	R	A	P
M	J	N	A	E	J	W	D	R	A	I	N	B	U	C	E	O
Z	C	O	S	C	R	B	A	E	M	O	I	W	X	U	E	R
P	R	E	N	A	G	O	Z	D	L	N	K	F	N	U	O	T
B	D	O	C	T	O	R	I	N	S	I	C	E	O	T	I	A
O	R	D	W	G	O	K	F	U	E	A	V	Z	W	S	K	N
H	I	Y	F	C	E	L	T	R	S	A	S	E	M	I	K	T
M	Y	W	G	O	S	E	V	S	Z	F	H	I	R	J	K	P
U	N	P	A	T	E	R	C	E	I	A	L	S	V	Y	X	E
D	Q	I	U	R	E	D	J	I	A	V	E	P	Y	O	Y	R
P	Z	I	T	W	J	B	O	U	L	E	V	A	R	D	K	S
L	O	S	K	A	Q	U	W	I	Z	C	Y	C	H	G	I	O
F	D	I	D	S	W	E	R	B	I	N	P	V	E	U	L	N

Make a Weather Station:
Raindrops Keep Falling

Adult supervision is recommended.

Rain and other forms of precipitation are a vital part of our weather. We depend on rain and snow to help maintain our supply of fresh water. Too much or too little precipitation can cause serious problems for everyone, so keeping track of rainfall is important.

You might be surprised to learn that amounts of rain can vary even in areas near each other. You might get 1 in. (2.5 cm) of rain in a sudden shower, and someone a mile away might not get a drop. You can make a rain gauge for your weather station that will keep track of rainfall for you.

Materials

clear glass or plastic or jar,
    at least 5 in. (12.7 cm) tall
plastic wrap or bag
waterproof tape, such as duct
    tape or electrical tape
scissors

Directions

1. Cut out the rain-gauge ruler shown on this page. Tape the ruler to the outside of the glass. Be sure to put the bottom of the ruler exactly even with the inside bottom of the jar.

2. Cover the ruler with plastic wrap and tape the plastic securely. Make sure you can read the numbers clearly.

3. Keep the rain gauge outside your weather station box. Put it where nothing is overhead, such as the edge of a roof, tree branches, wires or other things that could affect the amount of water that goes into the gauge.

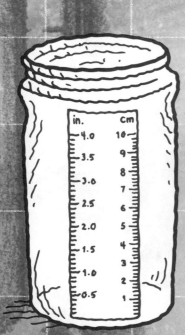

in.	cm
4.0	10
3.5	9
	8
3.0	7
2.5	6
2.0	5
1.5	4
	3
1.0	2
0.5	1

4. Record the amount of rain in inches and tenths of inches in your weather journal daily. After you have recorded the rain measurement, empty the gauge and return it to its proper place.

5. At the end of each week, graph your results.

Extension

Earth's waters move continuously from the oceans, to the land, to the air, and back to the oceans. This constant circulation of water is known as the *water cycle*. Research the water cycle at your local library, and then illustrate the process in the space below.

MATH CROSSWORD

Try to solve this puzzle using your math skills!
The example is bolded to help you get started!

Across:

1. Half of 6 across

3. Its digits add to seven

4. (18 across divided by 3) - 2

6. 11 across plus 18 across

8. 1 + (13 across - 6 across)

10. 1 down divided by 2

11. 10 across times 17 down

12. 16 down - 20

13. The square of 2 down

14. 6 across + 17 down

15. 18 across - last 2 digits in 6 down

17. Its digits add to 9

18. 6 x 17 across

Down:

1. 3 x 17 down

2. Twice 16 down

3. 11 across x 1 down^2

5. 11 across^2 times 17 down

6. One-fourth of 500

7. Its digits multiply to 64

8. 7 down + 17 down -1

9. 11 across divided by 3

16. The square of six

17. 1/2 of 16 down

PROBABILITY

Probability is the chance that something will happen.

It is expressed as a ratio. Match the probability statement with the correct ratio.

Finding vowels within the alphabet   **1 : 2**

Tossing a coin and turning up heads or tails   **1 : 4**

Finding consonants within the alphabet   **5 : 26**

Drawing a heart from a deck of cards   **21 : 26**

Journal

NOTE: If you need more room, use a blank sheet of paper.

TUESDAY

You are an alien who lives in a different galaxy. Write a letter to your pen pal on Earth.

_____

_____

_____

_____

_____

_____

_____

_____

_____

MEGA MATH

Can you replace the "?" with the right sign to equal 1?

Your choices are "+," "X," and "–."

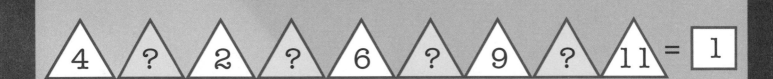

4 ? 2 ? 6 ? 9 ? 11 = 1

Parental supervision is recommended.

Toasted Peanut Butter and Apple Sandwiches

Ingredients:

peanut butter
one green apple
bread

Equipment:

toaster
knife

Directions:

Carefully slice the apples vertically about 1/2 to 1/4 inch (1-1.5 cm) thick (the thinner the better). Continue until you have four or more slices. Toast your bread and when it is done, spread peanut butter on both slices. Put your apple slices on so that they cover one of the slices of bread. Put the slices together and eat up! Only the brave will try this one!

Games   Phone Book Drama

- Materials needed: yellow pages, white pages, pencils and paper.
- Each player points to a name in the white pages.
- Write down the name, address and phone number. What city does this person live in?
- Now, open the yellow pages, and point to something with your eyes closed. Open your eyes, this is where your person works!
- Create a short skit using these people and their jobs as characters and places of employment.
- Think about what they would wear, what they would say and do.

THE MYSTERY OF THE LOST TIME CAPSULE

Chapter 9

Cody, Peyton and Klugh marched off to the Middletown Town Hall. If they could find the deed to Josiah Warner's property, they would be closer to proving that his was the oldest house in town.

They followed the signs to the property records department. Ms. Townsend, Cody's neighbor, was the manager.

"Hi, Cody. What can I do for you?" Ms. Townsend asked.

"We're looking for the deed to Mr. Warner's property down on River's Edge Road," said Cody. "We want to see whether it's the oldest building in town, so we can find the time capsule and win the bicentennial contest."

"I'd love to help you," said Ms. Townsend, "but there are no records before 1910. That's why there is a contest to find the time capsule. The records were lost in the Great Storm of 1910."

"The Great Storm of 1910?" Klugh asked.

"It was the mightiest storm this area has ever seen," Ms. Townsend said. "The wind blew so hard that the rain came down sideways. Trees were uprooted all over town, and lightning struck the church steeple, the gazebo in the town square, and the town hall. All three buildings burned to the ground. The town lost all of its records that night."

Peyton turned to her friends. "Then how can we prove that we have discovered the oldest house?" she asked.

"We'll have to look for more evidence," said Cody.

The three detectives trekked back to Mr. Warner's house, thinking about the storm.

"Back again?" asked Mr. Warner. This time he actually had a smile on his face.

Cody told Mr. Warner what they had learned. He lifted the old wooden box and said, "If only this box could tell us something."

"Hold the box still," said Klugh. "There's something nailed to the bottom of it."

Mr. Warner laid the items in the box on the table and turned the box over. There, nailed to the bottom of the oak box, was a small brass plate. "Something's written on it," he said, "but I can't make it out."

"I know how we can read it," Peyton said. "We'll do a brass rubbing."

ACTIVITY 9

Skill: Reading Comprehension—
Compare and Contrast

Cody, Peyton and Klugh are learning what Middletown was like more than 100 years ago. Think about the ways that Middletown has changed since the time capsule was buried. List the differences in the chart below.

Middletown Then:

Houses _____

_____

Clothing _____

_____

Daily Life _____

_____

Middletown Now:

Houses _____

_____

_____

Clothing _____

_____

_____

Daily Life _____

_____

Question and Answer

This smart-aleck cartoon character is the only one to have won an actual Academy Award.

Who is it?

FACTOID

Botanists work in a specialized area of biology that deals with plants.

grid LOGIC

Lativa and her three friends occasionally stop at Reynold's Drugstore on their way home from school to buy candy. From the following clues, can you determine each child's first and last name and which type of candy they purchased?

	Lativa	Erica	Chad	Lincoln	Jaw Breaker	Chewing Gum	Chocolate	Licorice
Donahue								
O'Connor								
Harris								
Green								
Jaw Breaker								
Chewing Gum								
Chocolate								
Licorice								

For examples and instructions on how to complete Grid Logic, turn to the back of the book.

1. Both Erica and the Green child are allergic to chocolate.

2. Lativa, the Donahue boy, and the girl who bought the licorice sometimes ride bikes together on the weekends.

3. Neither Lincoln nor the O'Connor boy purchased the jaw breaker.

4. Chad has braces and isn't allowed to chew gum.

Weird Science

Soap Bubble Physics

There's something great about blowing bubbles, but there's also something intensely strange. Why should individual bubbles always be round, and how do they connect to wands and each other the way they do? Stir up some bubbles for yourself and see.

You will need: liquid bubble blower, dish detergent or bubble bath, two bowls, a wire whisk or egg beater, some plastic bubble wands, chenille pipe cleaners, large paper clips, water, a straight pin, pepper or flour

Whipping Things Into Shape:

• Out of doors, slowly pour some bubble blower, detergent or bubble bath into a bowl, and stir it once slowly with the whisk or beater. What do you see? Stir the liquid very quickly. What do you see?

• Blow bubbles with a plastic wand. What is their shape?

• Bend the pipe cleaners into squares, triangles, and other shapes. Use them as bubble wands and blow one large bubble with each. What are their shapes?

An Invisible Skin:

• Fill a small bowl with water. Gently lay a straight pin onto the water's surface. What happens? Take the pin out and this time drop it into the bowl. What happens?

• Tap some pepper grains or flour particles onto the water's surface. What do they do?

• Dip your finger in bubble or dish liquid. Touch the water's surface. The plain water has a greater surface tension than the soapy water, so it pulls on the surface water (and the grains). What happens to the pepper?

Bubble Catchers:

• Bend some paper clips into bubble wands. Blow bubbles with one, then try to catch them with another. What happens? Dip two paper clip wands in bubble liquid. Blow bubbles with one, and try catching with the wet one.

• Try catching the bubbles with a pipe cleaner wand. Try catching one with soapy hands. Which surfaces catch the bubbles without breaking them? Think surface tension.

A bubble is a ball of soapy liquid filled with air. Bubble bath flows from a bottle as a liquid. It's the act of forcing in air that creates the bubbles, and it's surface tension that gives the bubbles their shape—water molecules pull together strongly at a surface, whether in a bowl or on a bubble. Bubbles also take on the shape with the least possible surface area—a sphere (a really cool fact for physics and math!).

Bubbles pop when all the air inside has evaporated. Compare how long bubbles last on a hot, dry day as opposed to a humid day (or just after it has rained).

> ## Remember to use the Scientific Method!
>
> 1) Make your hypothesis.
>
> 2) Record your observations.
>
> 3) Draw your conclusions.

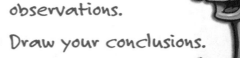

READING A BAR GRAPH

Answer the questions by reading the bar graph.

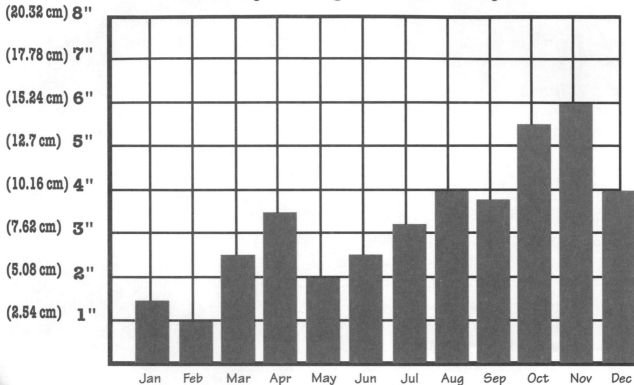

Monthly Average Rainfall - City X

1. How much rainfall did City X average in April? _____

2. During what month did City X receive the
   most rain? _____

3. During what month did City X receive the
   least rain? _____

4. How many months did City X receive two or
   more inches (5 cm) of rainfall? _____

5. How many months did City X receive less than
   two inches (5 cm) of rainfall? _____

Can you get through the maze and have less than 23 points?

Add the numbers and symbols as you go!

● = +5   ★ = -10   ■ = -5

START

20 ● 8 ★ 1 ★ 5

7 ★ 10 ■ 8 4

3 ■ 4 ● 5 ● 6

5 ★ 1 ★ 8 ● 10

FINISH

CROSSWORD

How well do you know analogies?

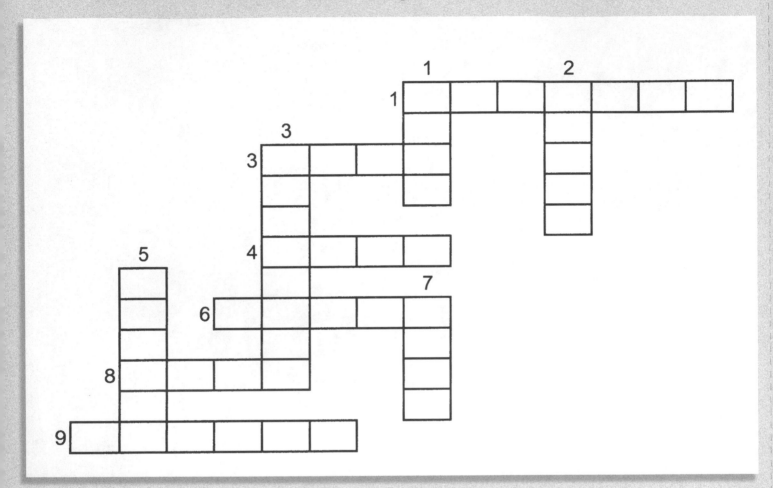

Across:

1. _____ is to stylist as surgery is to doctor.

3. Hot is to cold as up is to _____.

4. Square root of 81.

6. Sides on an octagon.

8. Hammer is to _____ as drill is to screw.

9. Dollar is to U.S. as peso is to _____.

Down:

1. Foot is to shoe as _____ is to glove.

2. Beat is to beet as write is to _____.

3. Uphill is to _____ as uptown is to downtown.

5. Paris is to _____ as Ottawa is to Canada.

7. Me is to you as us is to _____.

VOCABULARY QUIZ

Circle the word that matches the definition.

1. **flew**   virus

   flu

2. **flair**   style, elegance

   flare

3. **grate**   annoy, irritate or shred
                  (cheese for example)
   great

4. **currant**   recent, up to date

   current

5. **foreword**   comments written by book author,
                  found at beginning of book
   forward

Make a Weather Station:
Make a Cloud

Adult supervision is recommended.

Clouds are tiny droplets of water or ice in the air. Clouds form as moist air rising from Earth meets cooler air above.

Different types of clouds form according to the amount of moisture in the air and how that air may be moving or changing. There are many types of clouds, but the three main types are *stratus, cirrus* and *cumulus* clouds. Sometimes clouds seem to be a mixture of cloud types, so the name of the cloud is mixed, too. For example, cirrostratus clouds are a mixture of cirrus clouds and stratus clouds.

Another word sometimes used in cloud names is *nimbus.* This word means "rain," and the rain may pour from great heaps of *cumulonimbus* clouds (cumulus clouds that produce rain) or drizzle steadily from *nimbostratus* clouds (stratus clouds that produce rain).

Use the chart shown on the next page. Notice the type of weather that comes with each type of cloud. As you record in your daily weather journal, add information about what kind of weather you are having and what type of cloud you see.

Materials

glass jar
warm water

metal pan or tray
ice cubes

Directions

1. Put the tray in the freezer for a few minutes. The tray should be very cold before you begin. Put ice cubes in the metal pan or tray.

2. Put 1 to 2 in. (2.5 to 5.1 cm) of very warm water in the jar.

3. Place the tray of ice on top of the mouth of the jar.

4. Watch as the warm air rises from the water and meets the cold air dropping from the tray. Tiny droplets of water form in the jar, just as they do in the sky. The droplets may cling to the side of the jar, but they are in the air as well. Illustrate these findings in your weather journal.

5. You may see water from the cloud drop into the water below or run down the side of the jar. Your cloud is raining!

Cloud Types

Stratus	Thick or thin, low, flat layered clouds	
Cirrus	Thin and wispy, high, sometimes curly clouds	
Cumulus	Puffy and rounded, often piled up, low or high	

Extension

Precipitation can take the form of rain, snow, sleet or hail. Find the meaning of each type of precipitation by using a dictionary, an encyclopedia, or a web site such as www.weather.com. Write each word and its definition on the lines below.

_____

_____

_____

_____

_____

_____

MATH CROSSWORD

Try to solve this puzzle using your math skills!
The example is bolded to help you get started!

Across:

3. 5 across minus 11 across

5. 14 across^2

7. Its square is 169

8. 14 across x 17 down

10. One-ninth 26 across

11. First digit is twice the second digit

13. Its digits add to 2

14. Half of 21 down

15. Three times 18 across

16. 21 down x 3

18. 7 across + 14 across

20. Its digits add to 10

21. The square of 16

23. (20 across - 14 across) x 4

24. 19 down minus 21 across

26. Ten times 4 down

Down:

1. 19 down divided by 5 down

2. 7 x 14 across

3. 13 across times 14 across

4. 1/2 times 16 across

5. One-fourth of 10 across

6. 11 across squared

9. Its digits add to 13

12. 21 across minus 5 across

13. 20 across x (16 across ÷ 9)

16. 3 down plus 8 across

17. 5 x 13 across

19. 7 across times 10 across

21. Second digit is twice the first

22. 2 down - 11 across

25. Three times 11 across

27. The product of 7 across and 5

VERB TENSES

Circle past, present or future to identify
the verb tense used in each sentence.

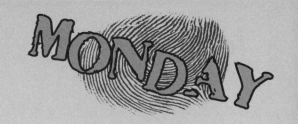

1. My Uncle Bill lives on a horse ranch.
   past   **present**   **future**

2. We will go to the beach next weekend.
   past   **present**   **future**

3. I ran all the way home from school.
   past   **present**   **future**

4. That dog barks every day at the same time.
   past   **present**   **future**

5. I will ask my parents if I can go.
   past   **present**   **future**

6. The chocolate chip cookies smelled wonderful.
   past   **present**   **future**

7. I will be in the 5th grade this fall.
   past   **present**   **future**

8. I completed the 4th grade in the spring.
   past   **present**   **future**

Journal

TUESDAY

What are some things you like to do with your friends?

_____

_____

_____

_____

_____

_____

_____

_____

_____

_____

MEGA MATH

Can you replace the "?" with the right sign to equal 30?

Your choices are "+," "x," "÷" and "–."

24 ? 6 ? 3 ? 2 ? 20 = 30

Recipes

Parental supervision is recommended.

Chocolate Cookie Flapjacks

Ingredients:

2 eggs
1 cup of flour
a little more than a 1/4 cup of margarine
3/4 cup of sugar
a little more than a 1/4 cup of cocoa
1 tsp of vanilla
1/4 cup of vanilla frosting
1 tsp of salt

Equipment:

2 or more mixing bowls
measuring cup
frying pan
measuring spoons
mixing spoon

Directions:

Make a mixture of the cocoa and margarine (melted). Mix your salt and flour separately. In another bowl, beat your eggs and add the vanilla and sugar, then beat that mixture some more. Now add your margarine/cocoa mixture and your salt/flour mix to the eggs/vanilla/sugar mix and blend everything well. Warm your skillet over a medium temperature and drop small amounts (about 2 tbsp) of your mixture in the pan. They should flatten out and cook like pancakes. Cook about 1 minute for each side (TRY NOT TO BURN THEM!). After all the mix has been used, put your flapjacks on a plate and refrigerate them until they become hard. Take them out and spread the vanilla frosting on one side and put another flapjack on top of it. Enjoy!

Games MISS

- Players: two or more.
- Everyone starts counting in rapid order, but they must substitute "miss" for the number six and all multiples of six.
- The first player to make a mistake must drop out and the last one left is the winner.

THE MYSTERY OF THE LOST TIME CAPSULE
Chapter 10

Mr. Warner gave Peyton a small piece of white paper and a pencil. She placed the paper over the brass plate and began rubbing over it with the pencil. Misjiff jumped up on the table and watched. Slowly, words began to appear on the paper: *Middletown 1903*.

"The centennial date!" cried Klugh.

"Mr. Warner, your box of old family stuff is really the time capsule buried at the town's centennial in 1903," Cody said.

"I think he's right," Peyton said, handing the brass rubbing to Mr. Warner. "That means your house must be the oldest in town."

A wide smile spread over Mr. Warner's face. "Imagine that!" he said. "Let's see what's in this box besides the daguerreotype. I haven't looked in here since I was a boy."

Mr. Warner began pulling out the box's treasures, including gold coins and newspaper clippings from 1903. He showed Peyton a finely crafted beaded necklace. "This must have been made by the Cherokee," said Mr. Warner.

"What's this?" Klugh asked, taking out a small piece of yellowing paper.

Mr. Warner gently unfolded the paper. "This is very old," he said. "It is made of rag, the material used for paper many years ago." He examined the paper and said, "It's a map, probably a settler's map."

"Look where the mark is," Cody said, pointing to the only X on the map.

The friends studied the map's squiggles and lines. The X that Mr. Warner had pointed to was located on the bend of the river. A letter *W* with a circle around it was next to the site.

"That X marks the spot where the Warner family settled," Mr. Warner said. "My great-grandfather must have carried this little map with him on his way west."

"This means your house had to have been the first house in Middletown," Cody said.

"Chee!" chattered Misjiff.

"Misjiff seems to think so," laughed Mr. Warner.

Klugh, eager to win the contest, said, "Let's call Professor Smith and show him all our evidence." Klugh grinned. "I'll bet we're the winners!"

ACTIVITY 10

Skill: Vocabulary—Word Jumble

Unscramble each set of letters to form six common words. Arrange the letters in the circles to make two new words in the boxes. The new words describe something important in the story. Use the hints if you have trouble unscrambling the words.

(A) G O (T) _____

Hint: a farm animal

N P (S)(I) _____

Hint: to turn around quickly

(C)(U) K L _____

Hint: good fortune

(P) A C (M) _____

Hint: to sleep in a tent

(E)(L) O S _____

Hint: opposite of win

C (E) N K _____

Hint: between your shoulders and your head

Question and Answer

This popular board game is made in 26 different languages.

What is it?

FACTOID

Because radio waves travel at 186,000 miles (299,338 km) per second and sound waves saunter at 700 miles (1126.5 km) per hour, a broadcast voice can be heard sooner 13,000 miles (20,921.5 km) away than it can be heard at the back of the room in which it originated.

grid LOGIC

Marian and her four friends each went to a restaurant to eat this past week. Based on the clues below, can you guess the first and last names of each child and the meal they ordered?

	Roberts	Peters	Bidder	Krill	Hawks	Hamburger and fries	Chicken	Swordfish	Steak	Vegetable soup
Alan										
Karl										
Kevin										
Marian										
Rob										
Hamburger and fries										
Chicken										
Swordfish										
Steak										
Vegetable soup										

For examples and instructions on how to complete Grid Logic, turn to the back of the book.

1. Neither Karl nor the Bidder child ate fish for dinner.
2. The Roberts girl, Rob, and the Peters boy take swimming classes together after school. The boy who ate the vegetable soup is afraid of the water and doesn't take lessons.
3. The Hawks child loves to put a lot of ketchup on his hamburger and fries, while Alan doesn't like ketchup at all.
4. The Peters child and the Hawks child's first names both start with the same initial, while Rob's last name starts with that same initial.
5. The girl who ate swordfish, Karl, and the Peters child all are in the same class as the child who ate the steak.

Weird Science

Making Wave Shadows
Create light waves that you can see as they interact with each other.

You will need: water, a flashlight, a shiny flat-bottomed pan or a tray lined with foil (the wider and deeper the better), a cardboard box big enough to fit over part of the tray, white paper, two sharpened pencils, scissors, tape, a small rectangular plastic box, a heavy mug, and mirror (optional)

Single Waves:

- Fill the pan with at least one inch (3 cm) of water. If you have a mirror, lay it flat in the water.
- Cut and throw away one long side of the box. Tape a sheet of white paper against the opposite long side. Place the box upside down over the tray, with the open side facing you.
- Hold the flashlight with one hand and shine it into the pan or mirror until you see the reflected light on the white paper. Hold it at different angles to get the best view.
- With your other hand, quickly dip a pencil tip into the water and then pull the tip out. Watch the reflected light on the paper. You will see the shadows of the ripples passing through the water in the same way as light (electromagnetic) waves pass through air.

Wave Collisions:

- Hold two pencils with your free hand, spreading them apart like chopsticks. Dip them both into the water; the ripple shadows created from the two points will collide and pass through each other as two separate waves.
- Put the small box in the water, weighting it down with the heavy mug. Dip the pencil into the water close to one side of the box, and watch the ripple shadows closely. Their shapes will change from circular to flattened rows as they try to go around the box's corner.

Wave Speed:

- Gently rock the pan and watch the waves bounce back from the edges. They'll even turn corners, reflecting from one side to the next.
- Rock the pan faster, and watch the shadows and patterns change more rapidly.

The faster the wave patterns, the higher the frequency of the wave. When waves of different frequencies collide they create a third wave pattern that is a combination of the two frequencies.

Tapping the pencils in the water creates spherical waves. Next time you throw a pebble in a pond, try two pebbles at the same time, and see if you observe the same types of interference patterns.

Remember to use the Scientific Method!

1) Make your hypothesis.

2) Record your observations.

3) Draw your conclusions.

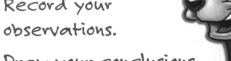

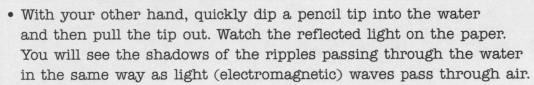

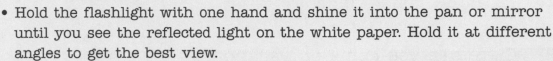

SENTENCE TYPES

A. Declarative sentences tell you something.

B. Interrogative sentences ask questions.

C. Imperative sentences give commands or make requests.

D. Exclamatory sentences express strong emotion.

Label each sentence with A, B, C or D according to its sentence type.

1. Oh, thank you so much! _____

2. Where are you going on vacation? _____

3. I really like to play baseball. _____

4. Come home right now. _____

5. I need help with my chores today. _____

6. Look out, there is a car coming! _____

7. Please call me later. _____

8. When can you be ready to leave? _____

Make your way through the maze and come out with the lowest possible number.

Add the numbers and dots as you go!

● = -5

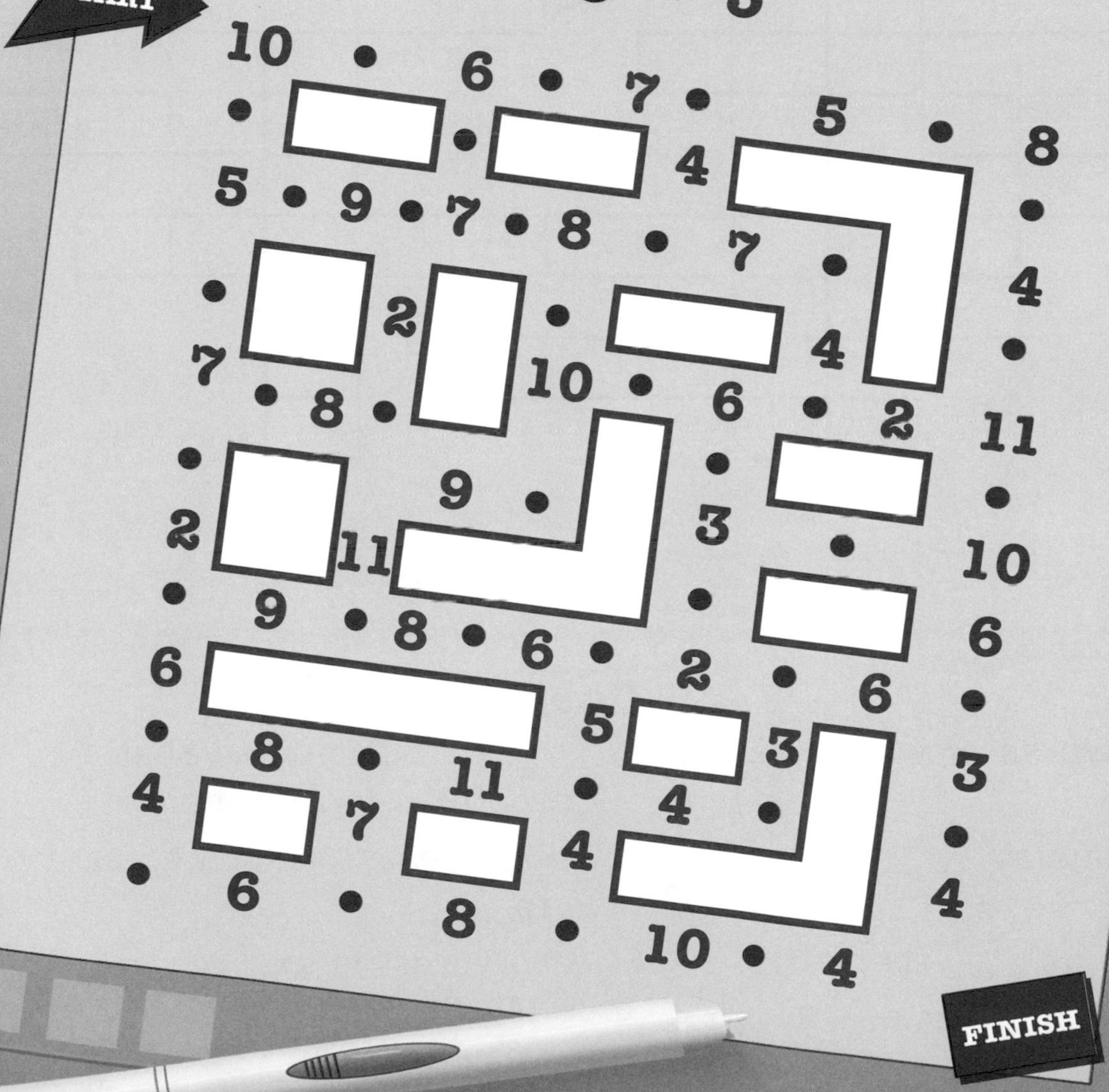

START

10 • 6 • 7 • 5 • 8

5 • 9 • 7 • 8 • 7 4 4

7 2 10 6 4 2 11

2 11 9 3 10

9 • 8 • 6 2 6 6

6 5 3 3

4 8 11 4 4

6 7 4 4

8 10 • 4

FINISH

CROSSWORD

How well do you know analogies?

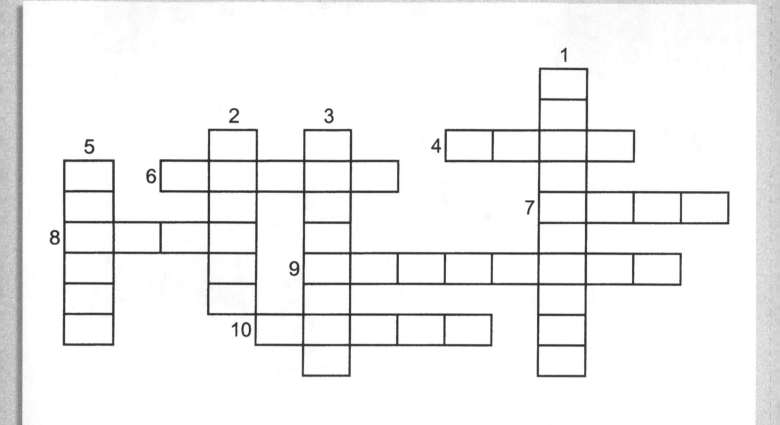

Across:

4. Deer is to fawn as cow is to _____.

6. Driver is to bus as _____ is to plane.

7. One is to two as _____ is to five.

8. 12 a.m. is to midnight as 12 p.m. is to _____.

9. Yesterday is to today as today is to _____.

10. Square root of 64.

Down:

1. _____ is to Pacific as South Carolina is to Atlantic.

2. Breakfast is to lunch as lunch is to _____.

3. Mt. Everest is to _____ as Mt. St. Helens is to volcano.

5. _____ is to lead as pen is to ink.

GEOMETRY: CIRCLES

Radius is a line segment from the center of a circle to a point on the edge of the circle.

Diameter is a line segment with both points on the edges of the circle. The diameter always passes through the center of its circle.

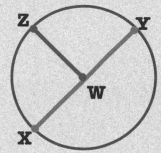

Radius = **WZ**

Diameter = **XY**

Label the radius and diameter for each circle.

1.

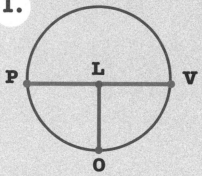

Radius = _____

Diameter = _____

2.

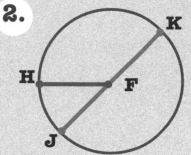

Radius = _____

Diameter = _____

3.

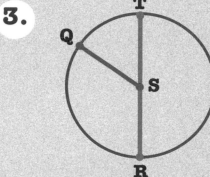

Radius = _____

Diameter = _____

4.

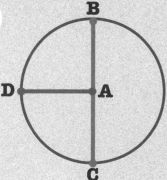

Radius = _____

Diameter = _____

Make a Weather Station:

Make a Hygrometer

Adult supervision is recommended.

Materials

wood, thick cardboard,
or foam, about
10 in. × 4 in.
(25.4 cm × 10.2 cm)
plastic coffee can lid
or smaller soft plastic lid
dime
3 or 4 strands of human
hair, about 10 in.
(25.4 cm) long
2 pushpins (not thumbtacks)
pencil
waterproof tape, such as duct
tape or electrical tape
scissors

Even when you don't see clouds or rain in the air, water is there. Moisture in the air is called *humidity*. You may feel hot and sticky on a very humid day, even if the temperature is the same as a less humid day.

Meteorologists measure humidity with a *hygrometer*. You can make a simple hygrometer if someone with long hair will let you have a few strands.

Directions

1. Cut out the pointer pattern from this page. Trace the pattern on the plastic lid. Then cut out the plastic-lid pointer.

2. Cut a slit in the bottom of the pointer as shown.

3. Slide the hairs into the slit, leaving ends of about $\frac{1}{2}$ in. (1.3 cm) on the back of the pointer. Tape the hair to the back of the pointer.

4. Tape the hair to the front side of the pointer.

5. Tape a dime to the front of the pointer as shown.

6. Carefully use one of the pushpins to punch a hole on the left edge of the pointer. Use a pencil point to make the hole big enough to allow the pointer to move freely. Push the pin through the hole in the pointer and into the wood about $\frac{1}{2}$ in. (1.3 cm) from the left edge of the board.

7. Place the other pushpin about 1 in. (2.5 cm) from the top of the board and about 1 in. (2.5 cm) from the left edge.

8. Carefully wrap the hair around the top pushpin. Pull the hair tight enough to make the pointer face straight out (level) and to the right. Fasten the hair with tape.

9. With the pencil, make a small line at the place indicated by the pointer.

10. Set the hygrometer near a running shower or by a sink full of hot water. Wait a few minutes and observe the change. Mark the change with the pencil.

11. Take the hygrometer to a dry place. How did the hygrometer change?

_____

_____

_____

_____

12. Put your hygrometer in your weather station. In your weather journal, describe what happens as the humidity changes from day to day.

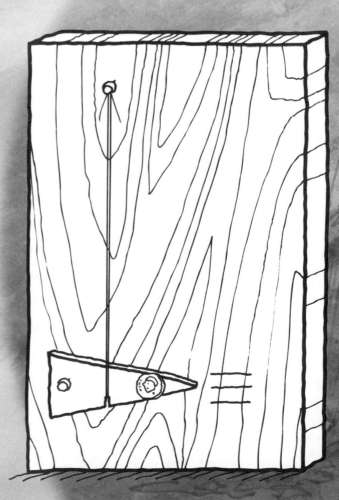

MATH CROSSWORD

Try to solve this puzzle using your math skills!
The example is bolded to help you get started!

Across:

1. One-fourth of 3 across

3. 12 across - 23 across

5. Double 13 down

7. 1 across minus 5 across

8. Its digits add to seven

10. 10 greater than (5 x 23 across)

12. 22 across times 10

14. 7 multiplied by 11 down

16. The square of 11 down

18. (5 across)²

21. Value of the 2nd digit in 23 across

22. 11 down - 15 down

23. 15 down squared

24. 8 across subtract 10 across

Down:

1. 16 down - 12 across

2. (Reverse of 13 down)²

3. Eight more than 3 across

4. 9 x 21 across

6. 16 across times 23 across

7. Digits are the same forward and reverse; add to 21

9. One-third of 5 across

11. Its first digit - second digit = 9

13. 3 x first digit of 12 across

15. The square of 4

16. 1 across + 12 across +1

17. Its digits add to 11

19. 3 down plus 23 across

20. The sum of 23 across and 2 down

144

SIMPLE ALGEBRA

Solve for the variable X in the equations below.

1. $10 = 2X + 4$ X = _____3_____

2. $X + 33 = 99$ X = _____

3. $100 \div X = 10$ X = _____

4. $36 - 3X = 6$ X = _____

5. $10X = 80$ X = _____

6. $22 + 33 + X = 100$ X = _____

7. $5X + 25 = 50$ X = _____

8. $44 - 11X = 0$ X = _____

Journal

NOTE: If you need more room, use a blank sheet of paper.

TUESDAY

Which would you rather have for a pet, a monkey or a dog? Why? _____

_____

_____

_____

_____

_____

_____

_____

_____

MEGA MATH

Can you replace the "?" with the right sign to equal 60?

Your choices are "+," "x," "÷" and "–."

80 ? 8 ? 9 ? 6 ? 12 = 60

Recipes

Petrified Worm Soup

Ingredients:
red and blue gelatin
gummy worms (red) or
another bright color

Equipment:
large mixing bowl
(preferably glass)

Directions:
Take your bowl and place the gummy worms at the bottom. Mix the gelatin packets together according to the directions on the package and pour mixture into the bowl. Refrigerate as directed. (You may want to pull some of the gummy worms up and have them hanging halfway out/in the bowl.) When the gelatin has turned solid pull it out and see if you can spot the worms in the bowl. Eat 'em up!

Games Everyday Creations

- Materials needed: everyday items such as safety pins, a comb, shoes, etc.

- Put all of the items in a big box or container and mix them up.

- Each player chooses an object, which they will study.

- Then, each player must develop a story about the item they selected. The story must illustrate a new and creative use for the object. For example, "This shoe may look like an ordinary shoe but it's actually one of the boats for the Grasshopper National Navy."

- This game is great for imagination and creative exercises!

THE MYSTERY OF THE LOST TIME CAPSULE

Chapter 11

The next morning Professor Smith studied the location of Mr. Warner's house with Cody, Peyton and Klugh. Misjiff ran along the top of the stone wall, as if to point it out.

Then Professor Smith went inside and studied the design of the house. He sat down to look at the box and its contents, spending several minutes studying each item. He was especially interested in the daguerreotype, the settler's map, and the brass rubbing.

While Mr. Warner watched silently, Cody, Peyton and Klugh fidgeted. Misjiff perched on Cody's shoulder, his eyes big and questioning.

Finally, Professor Smith said, "This is an *interesting* discovery."

"Did we win?" Klugh asked.

"There's good history here," said the professor, walking to the door, "but I have one other entry to look at today. I can't make a decision without looking at all the facts. I'll be in touch."

"Can you believe that?" Klugh asked. "He called it an *interesting* discovery!"

"I was sure we won," Peyton said, slumping down in a chair.

"Me too," Cody said.

Mr. Warner leaned his long arms against the table. "Don't give up!" he said. "The professor didn't say you won, but he didn't say you lost either. You've done some mighty fine detective work here."

"You'll go to the festival on Saturday, won't you, Mr. Warner?" Peyton asked.

Mr. Warner shook his head and said, "I don't like crowds. You can tell me how it all turns out." He placed the cookie jar on the table and said, "Have some cookies."

Later the friends walked home, uncertain about their chances of winning. As they reached Cody's front yard, his mother came running out. "Professor Smith just called to say that your team won the bicentennial contest," she said.

"We—we won?" Cody gasped.

"He said your research shows that Mr. Warner's house is the oldest in town. He believes that the wooden box is the original time capsule."

"We have to keep this a surprise for Mr. Warner," said Peyton. "But how can we get him to go to the festival?"

"Chee?" said Misjiff, sounding puzzled.

Skill: Reading Comprehension—Character Analysis

The character of Mr. Warner changes as the events of the story unfold. When you think about how a character changes, you are *analyzing* the character. *Analyze* the character of Mr. Warner, using the questions below.

What is Mr. Warner like when Cody, Peyton and Klugh first meet him?

_____

How does Mr. Warner feel about Misjiff?

_____

_____

What is Mr. Warner like near the end of the story?

_____

_____

_____

What causes Mr. Warner to change?

_____

_____

_____

Make a Prediction

Will Mr. Warner come to the festival?
Why or why not?

_____

_____

_____

Question and Answer

Can you name what travels at speeds up to seventy two million miles (115,900,000 km) per hour?

FACTOID

Rh factor, an antigen on some red blood cells, was named Rh because it first became known from the blood of Rhesus monkeys.

grid LOGIC

Cameron and his three friends each play a different sport after school. Based on the clues below, can you determine each child's first and last name and the sport that each child plays?

	Mike	Kiara	Cameron	Teresa	Soccer	Swimming	Basketball	Tennis
Phillips								
Neal								
Thomas								
Stallworth								
Soccer								
Swimming								
Basketball								
Tennis								

For examples and instructions on how to complete Grid Logic, turn to the back of the book.

1. Teresa, the Thomas boy, and Cameron all play a sport that uses a ball.

2. Kiara and her friend, the Neal child, ride home from practice together. The child who plays tennis and Teresa ride separate buses home.

3. Cameron thinks it's a pain that he has to put on shin guards before he plays his sport, even if they do keep him from getting hurt. The Stallworth girl is glad that all she has to wear are shorts and a T-shirt to play her sport.

Weird Science

Paper Magic

Shapes aren't always what they seem. Astronomers found that out hundreds of years ago, when they just couldn't figure how planets followed circular orbits. You can create the same orbital shape later discovered true for all space objects. And, with a little magic, you can also walk through a piece of paper, and see that not every object has both an inside and an outside.

You will need: paper on a pad, two pushpins, a piece of string, pencil, scissors, tape, and two different colors of ink pens

Creating Space Paths:

- Push the two pushpins into the pad of paper down the center, about two inches (5 cm) apart. Cut a length of string about six inches (15 cm) long, tie it into a loop, and place it over the pins.
- Using the pencil, spread the string out tightly, and run it along the inside of the loop, drawing a line as you go.
- Cut a longer string length, tie it, and draw around the pins again. Move one of the pins further away, and draw new shapes with the same lengths of string. Each shape is called an ellipse. What do the shapes have in common, and how do they differ?

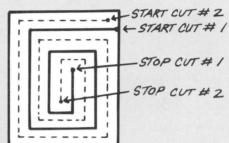

Walking Through Paper:

- Take a regular sheet of notebook paper and cut slits in a spiral pattern twice about one-half inch (1.3 cm), then one-quarter inch (.6 cm) wide.
- Unfold the paper completely—and walk on through. See diagram.

The Never-Ending Inside-Out Curve:

- Cut two strips of paper about one inch (3 cm) wide and 12 inches (30 cm) long. Tape two ends together to make one long strip.
- Take both free ends, one in each hand, and turn one end over so that the long strip has a twist in it. Now tape the free ends together to form a loop.
- Take one color ink pen, pick a point on the loop, and start drawing a line down the middle of the strip. When do you get back where you started? Take the other color and, starting at the same original point, start drawing in the opposite direction. What do you find?

In our solar system, the planets travel in elliptical orbits, with the sun at one side of the center, and nothing at the other side. Each of those locations, the same as where you put the pushpins, is called a focus, and both together are foci. The cut paper shapes are examples of transformed shapes that have wild math behind them.

The inside-out curve is called a Möbius strip. Try poking scissors through it and cutting along a dotted line all around the strip. How many strips, and how many sides, do you get?

Remember to use the Scientific Method!

1) Make your hypothesis.
2) Record your observations.
3) Draw your conclusions.

Journal

NOTE: If you need more room, use a blank sheet of paper.

Some things I like to do outside are...

_____

_____

_____

_____

_____

_____

_____

_____

_____

_____

OPTICAL ILLUSIONS

Stare at the black dot while blinking rapidly. After a while does everything around it seem to disappear?

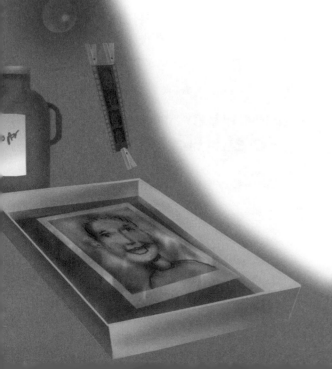

How many words can you find in this maze? All of them must start with the letter "s."

You may follow the letters in any order.

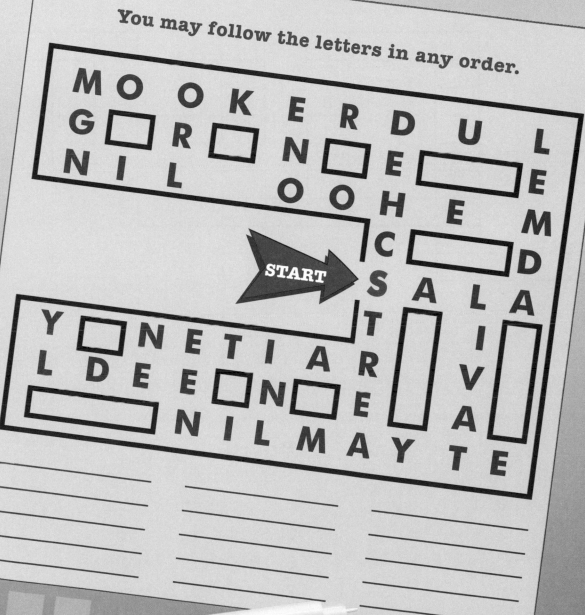

CROSSWORD

How well do you know your vocabulary?

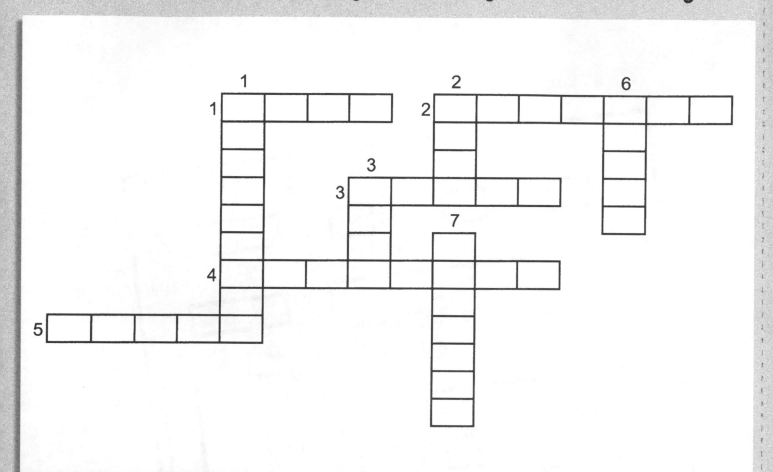

Across:
1. Homonym for deer.
2. Synonym for idea.
3. Synonym for odor.
4. Synonym for huge.
5. Antonym of loud.

Down:
1. Antonym of honest.
2. Homonym for tail.
3. Synonym for tart.
6. Homonym for grate.
7. Antonym of wrong.

FRACTION PUZZLE

Subtract diagonally to solve for A, B, C and D.
Then, add A, B, C and D together to solve for E.

A _____ + B _____ + C _____ + D _____ = E _____

Make a Weather Station:
Make a Barometer
Adult supervision is recommended.

Air pressure changes from day to day. Changes in temperature, humidity, and even the motion of air cause air molecules to move. As they move, air pressure changes.

Changes in air pressure usually mean changes in weather. High air pressure means that the air gets warmer as it is pressed down. Warmer air tends to keep clouds from forming. Low air pressure means that warm air rising from Earth will hit cold air as it goes up. Clouds will form, just as you saw when you made a cloud in a jar.

Air pressure measurements help predict the weather. Meteorologists use a *barometer* to measure pressure. You can make a simple barometer to watch air pressure change.

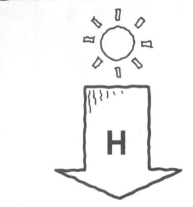

Warm air pressed down.
Clouds don't form.

Warm air rises to meet cold air. Clouds form.

Materials
clear jar
clear drinking straw
modeling clay

a few drops of food coloring
cold water
ruler

Directions

1. Fill the jar a little less than halfway with cold water.

2. Stir food coloring into the water. Be careful when working with food coloring as it can stain clothing or carpet.

3. Tape the straw into the jar so that it is in the water but does not touch the bottom of the jar.

4. Suck some of the water halfway up the straw. Pinch the straw, or hold it with your finger so that the water does not go back down.

5. Put modeling clay over the end of the straw (not letting the water level drop) to make an airtight seal.

6. Measure carefully the height of the water in the straw.

7. Each day take careful measurements of the height of the water in the straw. As air pressure rises, the water in the jar will be forced down, pushing up the water in the straw. This is high pressure. Good weather is associated with high pressure. When the pressure falls, the water in the jar will rise, and the water in the straw will fall. This is low pressure. Low pressure is connected to bad weather.

8. In your weather journal, record the type of pressure system based on your weather observations.

Extension

Look at the weather page in your local newspaper. What symbols are used to show the weather? Using an encyclopedia or a web site such as www.artandscience.org/sciencecenter/weather.html, find out what the symbols mean. Then, in the space below, draw each symbol and write what it means.

MATH CROSSWORD

**Try to solve this puzzle using your math skills!
The example is bolded to help you get started!**

Across:

1. Three times 9 across

3. 15 across - 16 down

6. (9 across - 1 down) - 1

9. 19 down²

11. 10 down divided by two

13. Half of 21 across

14. 10 x (15 across - 3 down)

15. 4 down times 19 down

17. (5 x 6 across) + 7

21. One full revolution

22. The product of 8 down x 19 down

Down:

1. Twice 16 down

2. 3 down minus 75

3. 16 down x the reverse of 19 down

4. 13 across - 6 across

5. Its digits add to 7

7. 324 x 1 down

8. 1 down minus 19

10. 3 down minus 13 across

12. (2 x 1 down) - 1

14. One-ninth of 13 across

16. Two times 19 down

17. 14 down x 16 down

18. 3 down - 1 down

19. A baker's dozen

20. (8 down - 16 down)²

PERIMETER

Perimeter measures the distance around something. To find perimeter, add the lengths of the sides.

Example:

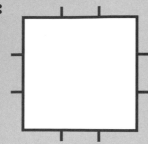

Perimeter = 3 cm + 3 cm + 3 cm + 3 cm = 12 cm

Solve to find perimeter in the word problems below.

1. The park's swimming pool is 12 meters long and 10 meters wide. What is the perimeter of the pool? _____

2. The public beach is 5 kilometers long and 2 kilometers wide. What is the perimeter of the beach? _____

3. The museum building is 500 yards long and 400 yards wide. What is the perimeter of the museum? _____

Journal

NOTE: If you need more room, use a blank sheet of paper.

You're sitting out in your back yard at night and you see a shooting star go by. What do you wish for? Why?

_____

_____

_____

_____

_____

_____

_____

_____

_____

_____

MEGA MATH

Can you replace the "?" with the right sign to equal 100?

Your choices are "+," "x," "÷" and "−."

46 ? 10 ? 6 ? 2 ? 4 = 100

Parental supervision is recommended.

Cranberry-Lemonade Juicesicles

Ingredients:
lemonade
cranberry juice

Equipment:
ice tray
plastic wrap
toothpicks

Directions:
Mix 2 cups of lemonade with one cup of cranberry juice. Pour into an empty ice tray. Cover the ice tray tightly with the plastic wrap. Poke the toothpicks into the center of each ice square. Freeze. Pull them out of the freezer, take the plastic wrap off, and enjoy on a hot day!

Homonyms

Each picture below sounds the same as one of the other pictures shown. For example: isle and aisle. Can you match up the pairs?

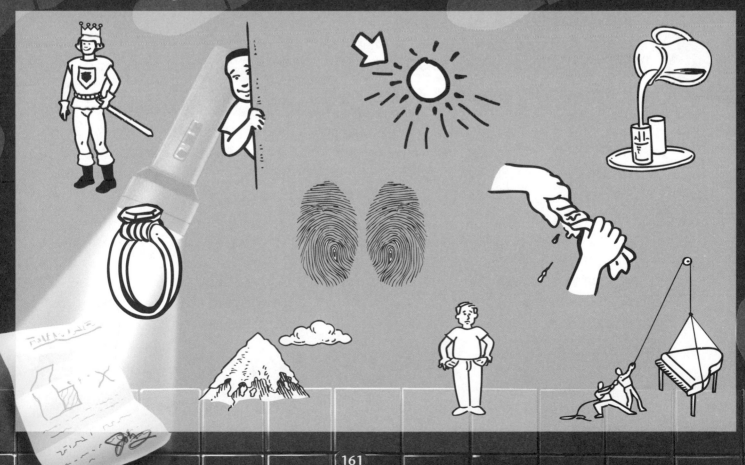

THE MYSTERY OF
THE LOST TIME CAPSULE
Chapter 12

Saturday morning at 9 a.m., Cody, Klugh and Peyton knocked on Mr. Warner's front door. Misjiff jumped to the windowsill and peered inside.

Cody called, "Mr. Warner, we've come to take you to the festival."

Mr. Warner opened the door and shook his head. "Thanks, but I told you, I don't like crowds."

Klugh said, "Mr. Warner, you're part of our team. Whatever happens with the contest, our team has to stick together."

"It won't be the same without you," Peyton said.

Misjiff sat down in front of Mr. Warner, gazed up at him, and said, "Chee?" It sounded like "Please?"

Mr. Warner's face softened. "I'm part of your team, am I?" he said. "Well—I guess I can't let my teammates down. Let's go!"

When the group arrived at the town square, they found it decorated with flowers, balloons and flags. A large crowd had gathered to hear the announcement of the contest winner.

"Ladies and gentlemen! Boys and girls!" the mayor began. "After careful consideration, Professor Smith has decided that the winner of the time capsule contest is—the team of Cody, Klugh and Peyton!"

The crowd clapped and cheered as the winners made their way to the stage. The mayor said, "The evidence is clear. The Warner home is the first structure in Middletown, and the wooden box is the centennial time capsule buried in 1903. The $1,000 reward goes to this team of young detectives."

"However," the mayor continued, "Cody, Klugh and Peyton have asked that the reward money be used to restore the Warner homestead."

Mr. Warner looked stunned. He paused for a moment and then stepped forward. "I am very grateful," he said, "but my friends plan to go to science camp. I can't accept the money."

"Yes, you can," said the mayor. "Our anonymous donor was so impressed by the kindness of these three kids, she's also sending them to camp!"

"Let's get a picture for the next time capsule," said a news photographer.

Cody pulled Mr. Warner next to him. "Sure," said Cody, "as long as you include the whole team!"

Cody, Peyton, Klugh, and Mr. Warner smiled for the camera.

Skill: Reading Comprehension—Story Response

Create Your Own Time Capsule

Middletown's time capsule contained items that showed what life was like in an earlier time. Suppose your town decides to bury a time capsule that will be opened in 100 years. What would your time capsule be like? What would you put in it?

Write a paragraph that describes your time capsule. Describe three items you would put in it, and explain why you would include each item.

Question and Answer

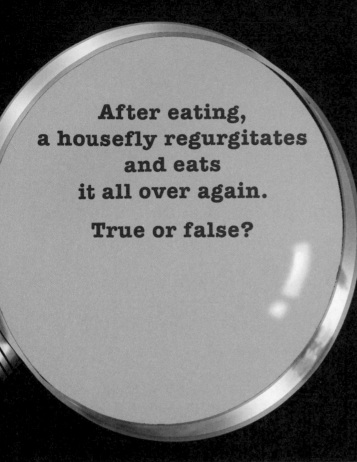

After eating,
a housefly regurgitates
and eats
it all over again.

True or false?

FACTOID

The Constitution is a ship that became famous during the War of 1812. Remarkably, it is still afloat and docked in Boston Harbor today.

grid LOGIC

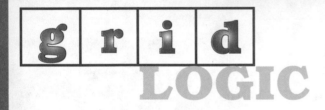

Keisha and her three friends went to four different movies. Based on the clues below, can you figure out each child's first and last name and the movie they went to see?

	Ethan	Dwayne	Caitlyn	Keisha	Space Invaders	A Dog's Tale	Western Round-up	Cartoon Capers
Gonzales								
Harrison								
Brunello								
Jefferson								
Space Invaders								
A Dog's Tale								
Western Round-up								
Cartoon Capers								

For examples and instructions on how to complete Grid Logic, turn to the back of the book.

1. Neither the Gonzales boy nor Dwayne likes space movies.

2. Keisha, the boy who saw "Western Round-up," Dwayne and the Brunello child all live on the same street.

3. The Jefferson child, who saw "A Dog's Tale," rode to the movies with Keisha, who saw "Cartoon Capers."

164

Weird Science

Magnetic Marvels

A moving magnet can make electricity, and a flow of electricity can make magnets—that's how electric motors and power door locks work. Use magnets as remote controls, compare their strengths, and see how their power can come and go.

You will need: various refrigerator magnets and any other magnets you have, paper clips, cardboard, facial tissues, a bowl, water, scraps of fabric, plastic cup, glass window or cup, small scissors, and straight pins

Magnet Motion:

- Take your assortment of magnets and try the following experiments. With thick, flat ones (round are especially fun), use one to push the other ahead along a tabletop. With a little practice, you can make the pushed one spin.
- Put one magnet on top of a piece of cardboard. Hold another magnet underneath, and see if you can move the upper magnet remotely. What kind of toy could you make with this arrangement (a moving car, boat or dancer)?
- Compare different widths and thicknesses of magnets by counting how many paper clips each can pick up.

How Tough Are Your Magnets?

- Try picking up paper clips while holding several folds of tissue between the magnet and the clips. Try again with the cardboard between them. Which magnets are strong enough to still work?
- Put a pile of paper clips in a bowl of water. Dip the magnets in the water. Do they still work?
- Try other materials between a magnet and a paper clip, or between two magnets: a thick cloth, a mitten, the sides of a plastic cup, a wooden paint stirrer, and a glass window.

The Changing Magnet:

- Try picking up a pin with the tip of your scissors (it shouldn't work). Now stroke the scissor blades with your strongest magnet, stroking in just one direction. Try picking up the pin again. Did it work? (Rapping the scissors firmly on a block of wood may reverse the process afterwards.)

Magnets are made from lots of different mixtures. An especially strong type is samarium cobalt, used to focus beams of electrons in cathode ray tubes (that's CRTs, as in computer screens and most TVs). Tiny strong magnets can even work through layers of skin. You can buy magnetic earring sets that have the look of pierced earrings, and doctors use magnets to change the control settings on surgically implanted heart pacemakers—without the need for going in with a scalpel.

Chemistry labs use cool magnetic stirrers to control mixing liquids. A small bar magnet is dropped in the glass beaker of liquid, and the beaker is placed on what looks like a hot plate. When the unit is turned on, a spinning magnet beneath the plate sets the bar magnet spinning, and you can control the speed of the mix.

Remember to use the Scientific Method!

1) Make your hypothesis.

2) Record your observations.

3) Draw your conclusions.

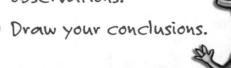

OPTICAL ILLUSIONS

Which inner triangle is bigger?

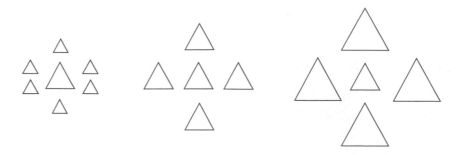

Are the long diagonal lines parallel?

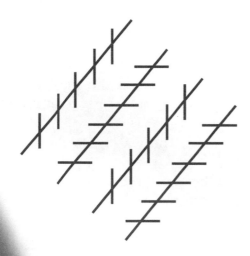

What do you see?

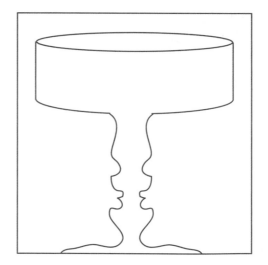

Do these shapes spell anything?

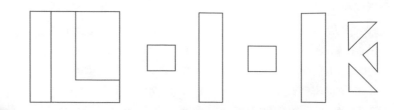

How many words can you find hidden in the letters below? Start at the arrow and follow the trail.

20 is good, 25 is great, and 32 is outstanding! You may have to use a dictionary for a few. (Don't forget 2-letter words, but do not count one-letter words.)

START →

B	R	A	N	D	E	D	U	C	T

E

A

C

T	E	R	I	T	E	R	E	H	C

A

I

L	O	R	D	I	N	A	R	Y	O

U

G

FINISH

L	L	I	R	H	T	H

CROSSWORD

How well do you know your vocabulary?

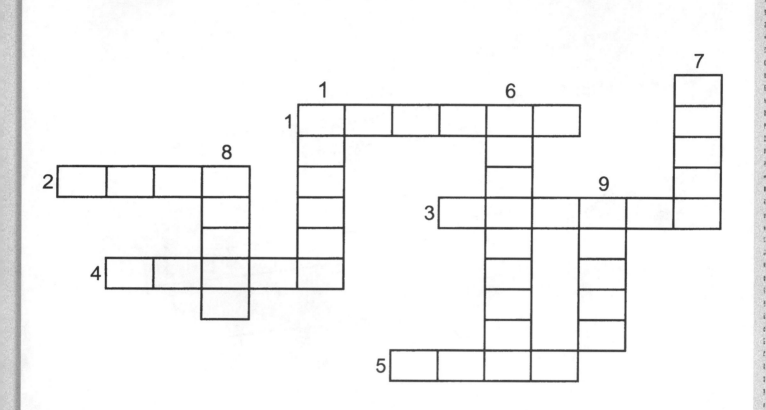

Across:
1. Synonym of dinner.
2. Homonym of bear.
3. Synonym of conclusion.
4. Homonym of their.
5. Synonym of cry.

Down:
1. Synonym of easy.
6. Antonym of cheap.
7. Homonym of lite.
8. Antonym of exit.
9. Antonym of over.

AREA

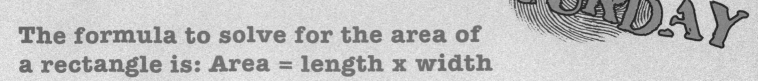

The formula to solve for the area of a rectangle is: Area = length x width

Example:

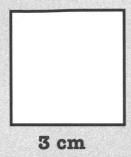

3 cm

3 cm

3 cm

3 cm

Area = 3 cm x 3 cm = 9 square centimeters

Solve to find area in the word problems below.

1. The park's swimming pool is 12 meters long and 10 meters wide. What is the area of the pool?

_____

2. The public beach is 5 kilometers long and 2 kilometers wide. What is the area of the beach?

_____

3. The museum building is 500 yards long and 400 yards wide. What is the area of the museum?

_____

Make a Weather Station:
A Weather Summary

Adult supervision is recommended.

As you finish your weather station equipment and continue making entries in your weather journal, you come to one of the most important parts of a meteorologist's job. You have collected many measurements, and now it is time to analyze your data. You can use the information you have gathered to help predict future weather. You will see that certain weather measurements *forecast,* or predict, upcoming weather conditions. For instance, cirrus clouds are signs of changing air currents; they tell you that new weather is on the way. A barometer reading is another example. If your barometer measurements are rising, or are high and unchanging, and the sky is clear with a light breeze, your local weather conditions should stay clear for many days.

Materials

weather journal notebook or binder with
$8 \frac{1}{2}$ in. × 11 in. (21.6 cm × 27.9 cm) paper
pencil

Directions

1. Make a three-column chart, and label the columns as shown on the next page.

2. Find the information for each column by reviewing the data in your weather journal. Record the new numbers in the three-column chart.

3. Remember how to figure averages. Add the totals first, and then divide by the number of observations. For example, a week's temperatures (Fahrenheit) might be 68 + 70 + 72 + 73 + 79 + 81 + 66 = 509. Then divide 509 by 7, the number of days, and get 72.7 for the average temperature. You will have many days to add, so it might be easier to add each week and then add the totals of each week together.

4. Figure average rainfall the same way.

5. Use the Beaufort Scale from page 59 to help you analyze the winds you observed.

6. From what you've observed, how would you describe summer weather where you live?

_____

_____

7. Keep using your weather station to make observations. Each day, try to predict what the weather will be tomorrow. Compare the measurements you take to those you get from the media. How do your observations compare?

_____

_____

Weather Condition	Data	Notes
High temperature and date	32°C, July 17	Hot week July 13—20
Low temperature and date	7°C, August 18	Cold snap lasted three days.
Average temperature	19.3°C	
Number of clear days	22	
Number of partly cloudy days	41	
Number of cloudy days	21	
Number of days of rainfall	18	
Most rainfall and date		
Total rainfall		
Average rainfall per observation period		
Number of calm days (wind less than 1 mph)		
Number of days with light winds (1—12 mph)		
Number of days with medium winds (13—31 mph)		
Number of days with high winds (32 mph+)		

Answers

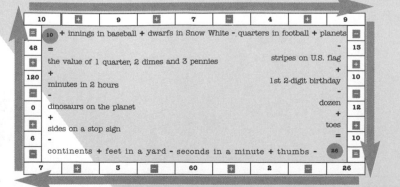

Monday page 4
VOCABULARY QUIZ
1. accept 2. effect 3. heir
4. choral 5. sight

Monday page 5
PLACE VALUES

1.

1,000,000s	100,000s	10,000s	1,000s	100s	10s	1s
卌 III	//	/	/	卌	卌	卌

2. 4,927,738

3. 989,011

4.

1,000,000s	100,000s	10,000s	1,000s	100s	10s	1s
///			/	卌 IIII	卌 IIII	//

5.

1,000,000s	100,000s	10,000s	1,000s	100s	10s	1s
卌 III	卌 II	//	卌 IIII	卌 III	/	卌 III

6. 6,900,604

7. 5,726,447

8.

1,000,000s	100,000s	10,000s	1,000s	100s	10s	1s
卌 IIII	/	/	卌 I	卌	III	III

Tuesday page 6
MEGA MATH

● = 6   ■ = 12

■ ■ ● ▲ = 34

Tuesday page 7
MATH IN A BOX

Wednesday page 9
ACTIVITY 1 - READING COMPREHENSION
1. Setting
In a small town called Middletown.
2. Characters
Cody, Peyton and Klugh are the kid detectives. Misjiff is Cody's pet ferret.
3. Plot
The mayor announces a contest to try to find the time capsule. Cody, Peyton and Klugh discuss what's in the time capsule and decide if they win, they will go to science camp.
3. Problem
The kids will try to find a time capsule barried in the oldest house in Middletown.

Thursday page 10
QUESTION & ANSWER
Digital Video Disc (DVD) Player

LOGIC PROBLEM
Tent. They all end with the first letter of the number.

Friday page 12
AVERAGING
1. 10
2. 20
3. 8
4. 5
5. 2.5
6. 40
7. 33
8. 7

Friday page 13
WORD MAZE

GLASS	BROKEN	STRING	STRONG	WORK	DOWN	THERE	SEAT
IN	OUT	TOWER	QUART	HOLD	HOUSE	LIGHT	SIDE
TIME	FRONT	END	HERE	OVER	FOR	TIME	IN
BUS	WASH	HIGH	WOOD	BOARD	GOOD	GOAL	TIME
DOORS	OUT	DROP	OUT	WALK	OUT	PLANE	HERE
OVER	ADD	BACK	RUN	SEE	SIDE	DARK	NIGHT
SPOT	ONE	SWEPT	WIND	DOWN	SHOW	AHEAD	WIND
PASS	FREE	ON	SLOW	SITE	DANGER	NOW	LIGHT

Week 1
continued

Saturday
page 14
CROSSWORD

```
              1
              M
  2 T I M E Z O N E S      3
              O            S
        4     N            H
        4 C A K E S        O
      5 |C|                E
      D |A|                S
      O |P|
  6 F U R N I T U R E      7
      N |T|                W
      U |A|                A
  8 B R I D G E S  9 S E A S O N S
      T |L|                S
```

Saturday
page 15
JOINING WORDS

1. because   4. so
2. or   5. but
3. after   6. when

Week 2
pages 18-31

Monday
page 18
QUOTATION MARKS

1. She screamed, "Get out of the way!"
2. "What did you say?" asked the teacher.
3. The waiter asked, "What type of salad dressing would you like?"
4. "Turn up the radio!" shouted Bobby.
5. "When will we be there?" asked the children.
6. Grandma asked, "Would you like some tea?"
7. Abby's mother reminded her, "Don't forget your sunscreen."
8. "Do you want to play baseball?" asked Susan.

Monday
page 19
MULTIPLICATION

1. 36,608   4. 75,522   7. 27,258
2. 8,064   5. 2,790   8. 2,490
3. 25,500   6. 45,486   9. 9,633

Tuesday
page 20
MEGA MATH

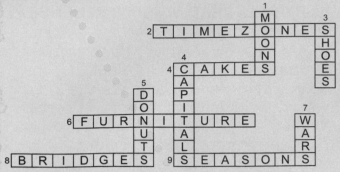

$$\triangle = 4 \qquad \bullet = 3$$
$$\bullet \times \triangle + \blacksquare = 17$$

Wednesday
page 23
ACTIVITY 2 - WORD STUDY

3 letters		4 letters	
ace	inn	ante	lain
act	lab	bait	lane
ail	let	bale	lent
ant	lit	bean	line
ban	net	beat	lint
bin	nib	belt	nail
bit	nil	bent	nice
cab	tab	bite	tail
can	tan	cent	tale
eel	ten	cite	teen
ice	tin	clan	tine
		lace	talc
			teal

Thursday
page 24
QUESTION & ANSWER
Currency

LOGIC PROBLEM

Nuts. They all begin with the last letter of the number!

Friday
page 26
DECIMALS

1. >   5. >
2. <   6. <
3. <   7. >
4. <   8. <

Week 2
continued

Friday
page 27
WORD MAZE

BACK	FLAG	OLD	BIG	TIRE	GOING	AGAINST	TOP
DOOR	HANDLE	BAR	REST	FORM	SIDE	BLUE	DOG
WEST	LEFT	BELL	CHIME	RED	ZONE	TRAIN	ZONE
SHIP	FRIEND	BOY	HARD	COLD	WATER	FALL	OUT
YARD	BOAT	GIRL	WORK	DAY	BREAK	OUT	BACK
STICK	LESS	SEAL	PIECE	SUN	QUICK	WALK	BOARD
PIN	BALL	GAME	TIME	RUN	LINE	OVER	PASS
CAT	BROWN	MICE	HOT	AIR	TREE	HEAT	PORT

Saturday
page 28
CROSSWORD

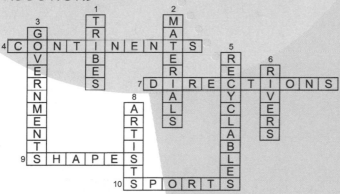

Saturday
page 29
PALINDROMES
1. mom   4. bib
2. Eve   5. did
3. noon   6. wow

Sunday
page 31
KEEPING A WEATHER JOURNAL

Weather: condition of the air during a brief period of time

Climate: the average weather of an area over a long period of time. Students' descriptions of their local weather and climate will vary but should reflect the definition of each term.

Week 3
pages 32-45

Monday
page 32
ANALOGIES
1. d 2. a 3. f 4. b
5. h 6. e 7. g 8. c

Monday
page 33
MONEY STORY PROBLEMS
1. $5.01
2. $84.00 tickets + $8.00 hot dogs
   + $4.00 soda pops = $96.00
3. $14.50 ÷ $.50 = 29

Tuesday
page 34
MEGA MATH

▲ = 10   ● = 2

Wednesday
page 37
ACTIVITY 3 - SEQUENCE OF EVENTS
3   1
6   2
5
4

Thursday
page 38
QUESTION & ANSWER
Leeches!

LOGIC PROBLEM
Fog. They all have the same number of letters as the number!

Week 3
continued

Friday
page 40
FRACTIONS

1. $5\frac{3}{6}$ or $5\frac{1}{2}$

2. $1\frac{4}{10}$ or $1\frac{2}{5}$

3. $1\frac{5}{8}$

4. $1\frac{5}{9}$

5. $1\frac{9}{12}$ or $1\frac{3}{4}$

6. $\frac{5}{14}$

7. $1\frac{1}{6}$

8. $3\frac{5}{10}$ or $3\frac{1}{2}$

Friday
page 41
WORD MAZE

PIT	FRAME	TOP	HAND	RAIL	WAY	ONE	KIND
SCORE	TRICK	WAGON	OFF	FIRE	OUT	TEAM	OLD
UNDER	FISH	WEIGHT	LIFT	CORK	BACK	WOMAN	HEAD
ONE	POINT	PAPER	LINE	BONE	DOOR	LIKE	RIGHT
CAP	STONE	WALL	CARD	BALL	BELL	HOP	SCOTCH
KNEE	BELT	TEST	GREEN	FOOD	OVER	RAIN	HINGE
AIR	PLAY	LEFT	DOG	CLEAR	LOG	SHIRT	CUB
NAIL	PEEL	LIGHT	CAN	SEAT	TOP	CHEESE	PLAY

Saturday
page 42
CROSSWORD

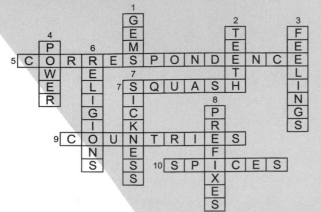

Saturday
page 43
IRREGULAR VERBS

1. did
2. sang
3. brought
4. drove
5. saw
6. slept
7. went
8. swam

Week 4
pages 45-59

Monday
page 46
YOUR vs YOU'RE

1. You're
2. your
3. your
4. you're
5. Your
6. You're
7. your
8. You're

Monday
page 47
DECIMALS

1. 1.1028
2. .4685
3. .5129
4. 1.1756
5. .2708
6. .8916
7. .0191
8. .4027
9. .8059

Tuesday
page 48
MEGA MATH

$$\triangle = 8 \quad \blacksquare = 2$$

$$\frac{\triangle \; \bullet \; \blacksquare \; \blacksquare = 9}{\blacksquare}$$

Wednesday
page 51
ACTIVITY 4 - SENTENCES

2. after
3. and
4. when
5. so that
6. but

Thursday
page 52
QUESTION & ANSWER
Mark McGwire

Week 4
continued

Thursday
page 52

LOGIC PROBLEM

Crayon. All end with the same letter as the number!

Friday
page 54

MATH SYMBOLS

1. ÷
2. ÷
3. x
4. -
5. x
6. +
7. ÷
8. x
9. +

Friday
page 55

WORD MAZE

BUNT	STITCH	JERSEY	SENSE	EYES	BASE	HERE	HOLE
OUT	GLASS	PITCH	RAN	GREAT	CALL	CHAIR	MAN
FLY	UMPIRE	TOP	NOTCH	TALL	LEFT	ARM	ERROR
HIT	WALK	PLAY	SECOND	MOUND	STEAL	SIDE	WIND
WIG	BASE	FACE	RING	HAT	HILL	TOP	OUT
GUM	SLAM	DRY	SEAT	SET	UP	FIRST	CAP
RUN	SIGN	UNDER	GLOVE	OFF	CENTER	SEASON	THIRD
SHORT	STOP	LIGHT	WEIGHT	LIFT	SCORE	INNING	LINE

Saturday
page 56

CROSSWORD

Saturday
page 57

THEY'RE, THEIR, THERE

1. There
2. their
3. their
4. They're
5. there
6. They're
7. there
8. Their

Week 5
pages 58-71

Monday
page 60

VERBS WORD SEARCH

finished, swim, navigated, swung, mowed, stared, appeared, laughed, baked, washes

		F	I	N	I	S	H	E	D		
						T					
	N	A	V	I	G	A	T	E	D		
		M			R					A	
		O			E					P	
		W			D			W		P	
		E		B				A		E	
S		D			A			S		A	
	W					K		H		R	
		U			S		E		E		E
		N		W			D	S		D	
			G	I		M					
				M							
	L	A	U	G	H	E	D				

Monday
page 61

GRID MAPPING

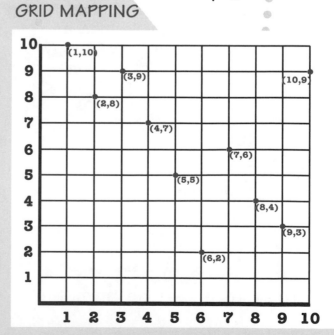

Week 5 continued

Tuesday   page 62

MEGA MATH

40 x	$1.00	40.00
40 x	.25	10.00
40 x	.05	2.00
40 x	.01	.40
		——————
		52.40

Wednesday   page 65

ACTIVITY 5 - READING COMPREHENSION
1. The men cut the trees for logs.
2. The house-raising begins.
3. The men carry and place the logs.
4. The women and children fill in the spaces with mud and clay.
5. The floors are covered with wooden planks.

ACTIVITY 5 - FOCUS ON THE MAIN IDEA
The book tells them what an early home looked like. It explains that it had a large hearth or fireplace, a thick door, and low ceilings. It also tells them that many early towns grew up next to rivers.

Thursday   page 66

QUESTION & ANSWER
pizza

LOGIC PROBLEM
Text. They all begin with the same first letter as the number!

Friday   page 68

EXPANDED NOTATION

1. **Words**= 5 thousands + 7 hundreds + 7 tens + 4 ones.
   Numbers= 5,000+700+70+4.
2. **Words**= 9 thousands + 0 hundreds + 1 tens + 1 ones.
   Numbers= 9,000+000+10+1.
3. **Words**= 8 thousands + 2 hundreds + 2 tens + 9 ones.
   Numbers= 8,000+200+20+9.
4. **Words**= 6 thousands + 1 hundreds + 5 tens + 0 ones.
   Numbers= 6,000+100+50+0.
5. **Words**= 4 thousands + 4 hundreds + 4 tens + 7 ones.
   Numbers= 4,000+400+40+7.
6. **Words**= 3 thousands + 9 hundreds + 8 tens + 3 ones.
   Numbers= 3,000+900+80+3.

Friday   page 69

WORD MAZE

HOSE	WATER	PINE	CONE	CAR	PEAR	IN	ORANGE
GRAPE	SOUR	APPLE	SAUCE	HOT	MILK	HOT	PITS
BUG	LEMON	SEED	PAN	FRY	FRENCH	PEEL	BANANA
BACK	RIND	WALK	CAKE	TIN	MAN	SKIN	SIDE
UP	BREAK	OUT	ANGEL	TIME	RACE	HUNT	MOTH
LIFT	LIGHT	BACK	HOUSE	WORK	HORSE	POWER	OUT
OFF	HAND	RAIL	ROAD	OVEN	PLAY	HOUSE	FLY
KIWI	ON	ANT	SIDE	BEE	BITE	BARN	PLANE

Saturday   page 70

CROSSWORD

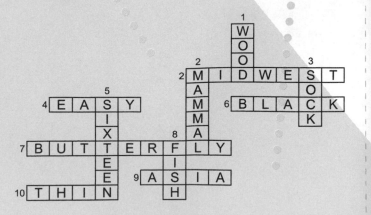

Week 5
continued

Saturday
page 71
ADVERBS

1. loudly
2. tomorrow
3. quickly
4. heavily
5. constantly
6. gracefully
7. clumsily
8. quietly

Week 6
pages 74-87

Monday
page 74
HELPING VERBS

1. (is) fixing
2. (should) begin
3. (will) change
4. (is) serving
5. (are) going
6. (might) enjoy
7. (will) stop
8. (can) play
9. (should) explain
10. (will) run

Monday
page 75
GEOMETRY: LINES, RAYS, LINE SEGMENTS

1. line
2. ray
3. line segment
4. line
5. ray
6. line segment

Tuesday
page 76
MEGA MATH

6 x	$1.00	6.00
6 x	.50	3.00
6 x	.10	.60
6 x	.01	.06
		9.66

Wednesday
page 79
ACTIVITY 6 - WORD RECOGNITION

Thursday
page 80
QUESTION & ANSWER
8-track tapes

LOGIC PROBLEM
Pen. They all rhyme with the number!

Friday
page 82
NUMBER SEARCH

1. 5,667,011
2. 369,339
3. 86,624,853
4. 672,756
5. 926,844
6. 1,218,576
7. 31,825,755
8. 3,601,515
9. 14,280,014
10. 62,477,403

Friday
page 83
WORD MAZE

Week 6
continued

Saturday
page 84

CROSSWORD

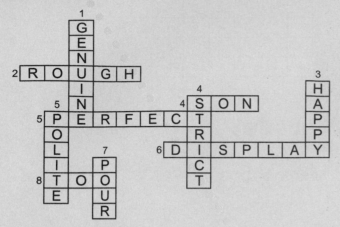

Saturday
page 85

VOCABULARY QUIZ

1. compliment   4. fare
2. confidant   5. hoarse
3. dessert

Week 7

pages 88-101

Monday
page 88

MATH CROSSWORD PUZZLE

¹1	0	²1	³0		⁴8	⁵1	7	⁶3
5		⁷3	0		⁸6	4		4
		⁹8	7	¹⁰2	1	7		
¹¹2	¹²8	7		4		¹³0	¹⁴0	8
	1						6	
¹⁵5	2	¹⁶5		¹⁷4		¹⁸5	7	4
		¹⁹1	²⁰2	9	²¹1	2		
²²8	²³7	2		²⁴0	4		²⁵3
²⁶2	0	2	0		²⁷5	8	6	5

Monday
page 89

FRACTION PUZZLE

$$A\ 1\tfrac{1}{10} + B\ \tfrac{9}{10} + C\ \tfrac{7}{10} + D\ \tfrac{9}{10} = E\ 3\tfrac{3}{5}$$

Tuesday
page 90

MEGA MATH

20 x $1.00	20.00
20 x .50	10.00
20 x .25	5.00
20 x .10	2.00
20 x .05	1.00
	38.00

Wednesday
page 93

ACTIVITY 7 - CRITICAL READING
DESCRIBING WORD

Cody
Possible answer: *smart*; makes decisions about what to do next

Klugh
Possible answer: *Clever*; remembers Ms. Carson's words; finds the right book at the library

Peyton
Possible answer: *cautious*; hesitates to go to the Warner house; tells Cody she won't go there

Misjiff
Possible answer: *curious*; runs ahead to the Warner house; runs up to Mr. Warner

Mr. Warner
Possible answer: *lonely*; lives alone; never sees people

Thursday
page 94

QUESTION & ANSWER
Capybara

GRID LOGIC

	Emily	Abigail	Tyrone	Matthew	Cat	Dog	Snake	Rabbit
Miller	X	X	O	X	X	O	X	X
Su	O	X	X	X	X	X	O	X
Baker	X	X	X	O	X	X	X	O
Evans	X	O	X	X	O	X	X	X
Cat	X	O	X	X				
Dog	X	X	O	X				
Snake	O	X	X	X				
Rabbit	X	X	X	O				

Answer:
1. Emily Su/Snake
2. Abigail Evans/Cat
3. Tyrone Miller/Dog
4. Matthew Baker/Rabbit

Week 7
continued

Friday — page 96
ADJECTIVE OR NOUN?

1. noun
2. adjective
3. adjective
4. noun
5. adjective
6. noun
7. noun
8. adjective
9. noun
10. adjective

Friday — page 97
WORD MAZE

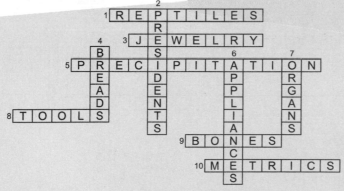

Saturday — page 98
CROSSWORD

Saturday — page 99
FACT vs. OPINION

1. opinion
2. fact
3. fact
4. opinion
5. opinion
6. fact
7. opinion
8. fact

Sunday — page 101
FAHRENHEIT TO CELSIUS CONVERSION

Measure Temperature Extension

Fahrenheit	Celsius
-31	-35
12.2	-11
33.8	1
53	11.7
78	25.5
86	30
101	38.3

Week 8
pages 102-115

Monday — page 102
MATH CROSSWORD PUZZLE

Monday — page 103
DECIMAL PUZZLE

Row 1. 1078.34
Row 2. 615.88, 462.46
Row 3. 338.42, 277.46, 184.73
Row 4. 176.82, 161.6, 115.86, 69.14
Row 5. 88.84, 87.98, 73.62, 42.24, 26.90
Row 6. 45.1, 43.74, 44.24, 29.38, 12.86, 14.04
Row 7. 25.2, 19.9, 23.84, 20.40, 8.98, 3.88, 10.16
Row 8. 15.6, 9.6, 10.3, 13.54, 6.86, 2.12, 1.76, 8.4
Row 9. 8.5, 7.1, 2.5, 7.8, 5.74, 1.12, 1.0, .76, 7.64
Row 10. 1.7, 6.8, .03, 2.2, 5.6, .14, .98, .02, .74, 6.9

Week 8 continued

Tuesday
page 104

MEGA MATH

9 x	$0.50	4.50
9 x	.25	2.25
9 x	.10	.90
9 x	.05	.45
9 x	.01	.09
		8.19

Wednesday
page 107

ACTIVITY 8 - ADJECTIVES—WORD SEARCH

B	C	S	T	B	G	E	W
Q	U	T	M	R	I	W	O
O	F	O	S	A	F	E	O
A	H	N	P	S	E	L	D
K	E	E	P	S	A	K	E
D	A	G	O	H	R	I	N
K	V	O	L	I	L	U	C
B	Y	R	D	N	Y	I	P
D	U	S	T	Y	F	C	D

Thursday
page 108

QUESTION & ANSWER
Michael Jackson/Thriller,
26 million copies

GRID LOGIC

	Alison	Cecily	Amir	Dominick	Super Reader	Space Voyager	Math Master	Adventure!
Parker	O	X	X	X	X	X	X	O
Bucetti	X	X	X	O	O	X	X	X
Alexander	X	X	O	X	X	O	X	X
DuBois	X	O	X	X	X	X	O	X
Super Reader	X	X	X	O				
Space Voyager	X	X	O	X				
Math Master	X	O	X	X				
Adventure!	O	X	X	X				

Answer:
1. Alison Parker/Adventure!
2. Cecily DuBois/Math Master
3. Amir Alexander/Space Voyager
4. Dominick Bucetti/Super Reader

Friday
page 110

MAKE A BAR GRAPH

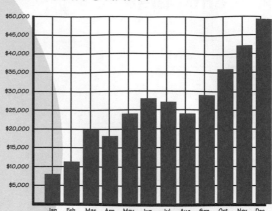

Friday
page 111

WORD MAZE

F	O	R	E	S	N	T	H	R	E	E	F	O
E												L
R	threefold		in		songbird		fore					D
E	three		rain		bird		for					E
H	fold		ain't		birdbath		or					D
T	old		taken		bath		ore					I
A	folded		take		at		bat					C
B	dedicate		kennel		bathe		reef					A
D	cat		nelson		the							T
R	ate		so		there							E
I	at		on		here							R
B	cater		son		therefore							R
G	terrain		song									A
N	O	S	L	E	N	N	E	K	A	T	N	I

Saturday
page 112

CROSSWORD

```
                        1
                        M
                        A
                        M
      2                 M        5            3
                        M                     C
   4  T R A N S P O R T A T I O N             O
      A                 E            L        L
   6  V E G E T A B L E S            S    7   O  8
      G                 A                  R O C K S
      U                 T                  S   O
      A                 I  9  F R U I T S       I
      G                 V                       N
      E                 E            10 E L E M E N T S
      S                 S
```

Saturday
page 113

ABBREVIATIONS

Registered Nurse, Doctor, Mister, Television, Street, Avenue, Very Important Person, Cash on Delivery, Road, Boulevard

Week 9
pages 116-129

Monday
page 116

MATH CROSSWORD PUZZLE

			5	6	7					
3	1	2	4		4	2	1	5	4	
4									2	
6 1	1	3	4		8	4	0	5	1	
10 2	7		11 4	8	6		12	1	6	
13 5	1	8	4		14	1	1	5	2	
7								2		
15 6	2	16 3		17	1	0	8			
	18 6	4	8							

Monday
page 117

PROBABILITY

Finding vowels within the alphabet-5:26
Tossing coin & turning up heads or tails-1:2
Finding consonants within the alphabet-21:26
Drawing a heart from a deck of cards-1:4

Tuesday
page 118

MEGA MATH

$$X, -, +, \div$$

Wednesday
page 120

ACTIVITY 9 - READING COMPREHENSION

Middletown Then
Houses: log cabins
Clothing: long skirts, big hats, suspenders
Daily Life: raised their own food, made everything themselves, walked or rode horses

Middletown Now
Houses: houses with siding
Clothing: shorts, women in pants, baseball caps
Daily Life: television, electricity, computers, cars and buses

Thursday
page 122

QUESTION & ANSWER
Bugs Bunny

GRID LOGIC

	Lativa	Erica	Chad	Lincoln	Jaw Breaker	Chewing Gum	Chocolate	Licorice
Donahue	X	X	X	O	X	O	X	X
O'Connor	X	X	O	X	X	X	O	X
Harris	X	O	X	X	X	X	X	O
Green	O	X	X	X	O	X	X	X
Jaw Breaker	O	X	X	X				
Chewing Gum	X	X	X	O				
Chocolate	X	X	O	X				
Licorice	X	O	X	X				

Answers:
1. Lincoln Donahue/Chewing Gum
2. Chad O'Connor/Chocolate
3. Erica Harris/Licorice
4. Lativa Green/Jaw Breaker

Friday
page 124

READING A BAR GRAPH

1. 3.5 inches (8.89 cm)
2. November
3. February
4. 10 months
5. 2 months

Friday
page 125

WORD MAZE

Answer is 22

Week 9
continued

Saturday
page 126
CROSSWORD

Saturday
page 127
VOCABULARY QUIZ

1. flu
2. flair
3. grate
4. current
5. foreward

Sunday
page 129
MAKE A CLOUD

rain: drops of water that are greater than 0.5 mm

snow: frozen ice crystals that usually are clustered into snowflakes

sleet: small pellets of ice that are less than 0.5 mm

hail: pieces of ice that are greater than 0.5 mm and vary in shape and size

Week 10
pages 130-143

Monday
page 130
MATH CROSSWORD PUZZLE

Monday
page 131
VERB TENSES

1. present
2. future
3. past
4. present
5. future
6. past
7. future
8. past

Tuesday
page 132
MEGA MATH

$$\div, \ \times, \ -, \ +$$

Wednesday
page 135
ACTIVITY 10 - VOCABULARY

Word Jumble				Answer:
G	O	A	T	TIME
S	P	I	N	CAPSULE
L	U	C	K	
C	A	M	P	
L	O	S	E	
N	E	C	K	

Thursday
page 136
QUESTION & ANSWER
Monopoly®

GRID LOGIC

	Roberts	Peters	Bidder	Krill	Hawks	Hamburger and fries	Chicken	Swordfish	Steak	Vegetable soup
Alan	X	X	O	X	X	X	X	X	X	O
Karl	X	X	X	X	O	O	X	X	X	X
Kevin	X	O	X	X	X	X	O	X	X	X
Marian	O	X	X	X	X	X	X	O	X	X
Rob	X	X	X	O	X	X	X	X	O	X
Hamburger and fries	X	X	X	X	O					
Chicken	X	O	X	X	X					
Swordfish	O	X	X	X	X					
Steak	X	X	X	O	X					
Vegetable soup	X	X	O	X	X					

Answers:
1. Alan Bidder/Vegetable Soup
2. Karl Hawks/Hamburger and fries
3. Kevin Peters/Chicken
4. Marian Roberts/Swordfish
5. Rob Krill/Steak

Week 10
continued

Friday
SENTENCE TYPES
page 138

1. D
2. B
3. A
4. C
5. A
6. D
7. C
8. B

Friday
WORD MAZE
page 139

There may be other correct answers.

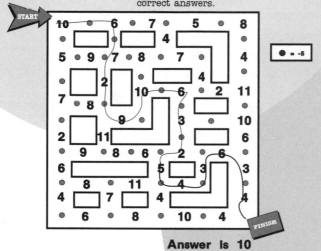

Answer is 10

Saturday
CROSSWORD
page 140

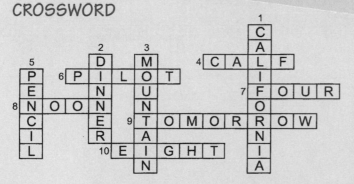

Saturday
GEOMETRY: CIRCLES
page 141

1. Radius=LO/Diameter=PV
2. Radius=FH/Diameter=JK
3. Radius=SQ/Diameter=RT
4. Radius=AD/Diameter=BC

Sunday
MAKE A HYGROMETER
page 143

Make a Hygrometer
11. When air contains a great deal of moisture, as it did near the shower, human hair cells expand. The strands get longer, and the pointer drops. When air is dry, the cells get smaller and the strands get shorter. The pointer rises.

Week 11
pages 144-157

Monday
MATH CROSSWORD PUZZLE
page 144

Monday
SIMPLE ALGEBRA
page 145

1. X=3
2. X=66
3. X=10
4. X=10
5. X=8
6. X=45
7. X=5
8. X=4

Tuesday
MEGA MATH
page 146

$$-, \div, \times, +$$

Week 11
continued

Wednesday
page 149
ACTIVITY 11 - READING COMPREHENSION

What's Mr. Warner like?
He is gruff and unfriendly.
How does Mr. Warner feel about Misjiff?
He likes Misjiff and feeds him peanuts. He likes animals.
What is Mr. Warner like near the end of the story?
He is becoming friendlier and talks with the kids. He is getting used to being around people again.
What causes Mr. Warner to change?
First, he responds to Misjiff. Then he responds to the detectives, especially when he finds out that his house is important in Middletown's history.

MAKE A PREDICTION
Will Mr. Warner come to the festival? Why or why not?
Yes, he will come. He likes the children now and he wants to find out what will happen in the contest.

Thursday
page 150
QUESTION & ANSWER
lightning

GRID LOGIC

	Mike	Kiara	Cameron	Teresa	Soccer	Swimming	Basketball	Tennis
Phillips	X	O	X	X	X	O	X	X
Neal	X	X	O	X	O	X	X	X
Thomas	O	X	X	X	X	X	X	O
Stallworth	X	X	X	O	X	X	O	X
Soccer	X	X	O	X				
Swimming	X	O	X	X				
Basketball	X	X	X	O				
Tennis	O	X	X	X				

Answers:
1. Mike Thomas/Tennis
2. Kiara Phillips/Swimming
3. Cameron Neal/Soccer
4. Teresa Stall/Basketball

Friday
page 153
WORD MAZE

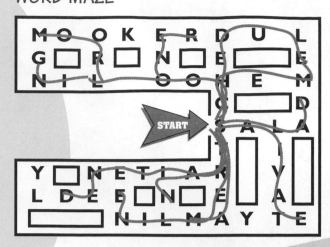

strait   schooner   salad
strain   schoolroom   saliva
stream   schooling   salivate
streamline   schedule
school   scheme

Saturday
page 154
CROSSWORD

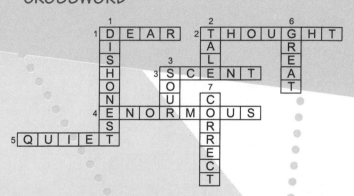

Saturday
page 155
FRACTION PUZZLE

$$A \frac{1}{2} + B \frac{1}{2} + C \frac{1}{3} + D 1\frac{2}{3} = E\ 3$$

Week 12
pages 158-171

Monday — page 158
MATH CROSSWORD PUZZLE

	1.5	0	7		3.8	0	4.6
	2		3		0		4
5.6			6.1	1	6		8.3
9.1	10.6	9		6		11.3	12.1	3
	2		13.1	8	0		0
14.2	6	0		4		15.8	3	16.2
0			17.5	8	18.7			6
	19.1		2		5		20.4
	21.3	6	0		22.4	2	9

Monday — page 159
PERIMETER

1. 44 meters
2. 14 kilometers
3. 1800 yards

Tuesday — page 160
MEGA MATH

$$+, -, \div, \times$$

Tuesday — page 161
HOMONYMS

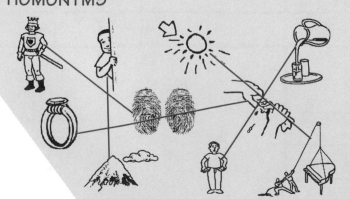

Thursday — page 164
QUESTION & ANSWER
true

GRID LOGIC

	Ethan	Dwayne	Caitlyn	Keisha	Space Invaders	A Dogs Tale	Western Round-up	Cartoon Capers
Gonzales	O	X	X	X	X	X	O	X
Harrison	X	X	X	O	X	X	X	O
Brunello	X	X	O	X	O	X	X	X
Jefferson	X	O	X	X	X	O	X	X
Space Invaders	X	X	O	X				
A Dogs Tale	X	O	X	X				
Western Round-up	O	X	X	X				
Cartoon Capers	X	X	X	O				

Answers:
1. Ethan Gonzales/ Western Round-up
2. Dwayne Jefferson/ A Dog's Tale
3. Caitlyn Brunello/ Space Invaders
4. Keisha Harrison/ Cartoon Capers

Friday — page 167
WORD MAZE

brand · teacher · ail
bran · he · lord
and · ache · or
branded · her · in
ran · here · ordinary
an · retire · nary
and · ire · you
deduct · tire · ought
duct · retail · thrill
tea · tail · ill
teach · tailor · rill

Saturday — page 168
CROSSWORD

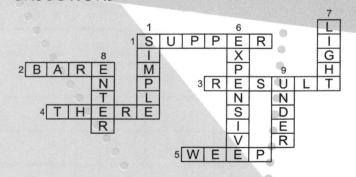

Saturday — page 169
AREA

1. 120 square meters
2. 10 square kilometers
3. 200,000 square yards

How to solve
Grid Logic problems...

Grid logic is a fun way to figure out what traits or facts should be paired together, based on a series of clues that have been given. The key part of solving a grid logic problem is the grid. As you read the questions, use the grid to mark with an "X" traits that you know don't go together. For example, if the clue is "Emily and the Phillips child live near each other," you can put an X in the box that pairs "Emily" and "Phillips" together, because you now know they are two separate people. Make sure to pay close attention to the clues that are given. For example, if the clue says, "the Turner boy..." you know to mark an "X" by any girl's name that intersects with Turner. The clue just told you that the Turner child is a boy, not a girl. If you know that two traits **do** go together, you can mark the intersecting box with an "O." The following is an example of a grid logic problem. Let's solve it together.

Mary and her friends went to the pool. While they were there, they each swam laps using a different stroke. Based on the clues below, can you determine each child's first and last name and the type of stroke they used?

1. Mary and the Waters girl both ride their bikes to the pool.
2. The boy who swam the breaststroke has the same initial for his first and last name.
3. The child who swam freestyle, Mary, and the Holland child all live in the same neighborhood.
4. Christopher swam a stroke named after an insect.

	Mary	Cecily	Christopher	Jon	Backstroke	Freestyle	Breaststroke	Butterfly
Jones								
Waters								
Holland								
Warner								
Backstroke								
Freestyle								
Breaststroke								
Butterfly								

1. Mary and the Waters girl both ride their bikes to the pool.

This clue tells us that Mary's last name is not Waters, so we place an "X" in the box that intersects "Mary" and "Waters." It also tells us that the Waters child is a girl, so we can also place an "X" in the boxes that intersect "Waters" with "Christopher" and "Jon" because they are not girls.

By doing that, it is clear that the Waters child is Cecily, so we can place an "O" in that box. We can also place an "X" in the boxes that cross Cecily with the other last names: Jones, Holland and Warner.

2. The boy who swam the breaststroke has the same initial for his first and last name.

The only first and last names that have the same initial are "Jon" and "Jones," so we can place an "O" in that box and an "X" in the others.

We can also place an "O" in the boxes that intersect "Jon" and "Jones" with "breaststroke."

3. The child who swam freestyle, Mary, and the Holland child all live in the same neighborhood.

This clue tells us that Mary's last name is not Holland. By placing an "X" in that box, we find out that Mary's last name is Warner and Christopher's is Holland.

It also tells us that Mary (Warner) and (Christopher) Holland did not swim freestyle. By crossing out those boxes, we discover that it was Cecily who swam freestyle.

4. Christopher swam a stroke named after an insect.

The only stroke named after an insect is the "butterfly" and this clue tells us that Christopher is the one who swam it. After matching "Christopher" with the "butterfly," we discover that Mary is the child who swam the backstroke.

The grid is now complete and it gives us these answers: Mary Warner swam backstroke, Cecily Waters swam freestyle, Christopher Holland swam butterfly, and Jon Jones swam breaststroke.

	Mary	Cecily	Christopher	Jon	Backstroke	Freestyle	Breaststroke	Butterfly
Jones								
Waters	X		X	X				
Holland								
Warner								
Backstroke								
Freestyle								
Breaststroke								
Butterfly								

	Mary	Cecily	Christopher	Jon	Backstroke	Freestyle	Breaststroke	Butterfly
Jones		X						
Waters	X	O	X	X				
Holland		X						
Warner		X						
Backstroke								
Freestyle								
Breaststroke								
Butterfly								

	Mary	Cecily	Christopher	Jon	Backstroke	Freestyle	Breaststroke	Butterfly
Jones	X	X	X	O				
Waters	X	O	X	X				
Holland		X		X				
Warner		X		X				
Backstroke								
Freestyle								
Breaststroke								
Butterfly								

	Mary	Cecily	Christopher	Jon	Backstroke	Freestyle	Breaststroke	Butterfly
Jones	X	X	X	O	X	X	O	X
Waters	X	O	X	X			X	
Holland		X		X			X	
Warner		X		X			X	
Backstroke				X				
Freestyle				X				
Breaststroke	X	X	X	O				
Butterfly				X				

	Mary	Cecily	Christopher	Jon	Backstroke	Freestyle	Breaststroke	Butterfly
Jones	X	X	X	O	X	X	O	X
Waters	X	O	X	X	X	O	X	X
Holland	X	X	O	X		X	X	
Warner	O	X	X	X		X	X	
Backstroke		X		X				
Freestyle	X	O	X	X				
Breaststroke	X	X	X	O				
Butterfly		X		X				

	Mary	Cecily	Christopher	Jon	Backstroke	Freestyle	Breaststroke	Butterfly
Jones	X	X	X	O	X	X	O	X
Waters	X	O	X	X	X	O	X	X
Holland	X	X	O	X		X	X	
Warner	O	X	X	X		X	X	
Backstroke		X		X				
Freestyle	X	O	X	X				
Breaststroke	X	X	X	O				
Butterfly		X		X				

	Mary	Cecily	Christopher	Jon	Backstroke	Freestyle	Breaststroke	Butterfly
Jones	X	X	X	O	X	X	O	X
Waters	X	O	X	X	X	O	X	X
Holland	X	X	O	X	X	X	X	O
Warner	O	X	X	X	O	X	X	X
Backstroke	O	X	X	X				
Freestyle	X	O	X	X				
Breaststroke	X	X	X	O				
Butterfly	X	X	O	X				

Answer:
Mary Warner/Backstroke
Cecily Waters/Freestyle
Christopher Holland/Butterfly
Jon Jones/Breaststroke

Wind Speed Answers

Force Number	Description of Wind	Effects On Land	Wind Speed MPH	Wind Speed km/h
0	Calm	Smoke rises straight up.	Less than 1	Less than 1
1	Light Air	Smoke drifts in direction of wind.	1-3	1-5
2	Slight Breeze	Wind is felt on face. Leaves and flags rustle.	4-7	6-11
3	Gentle Breeze	Leaves and twigs constantly move. Light flags extend.	8-12	12-19
4	Moderate Breeze	Dust and loose paper move, as well as small branches.	13-18	20-28
5	Fresh Breeze	Small trees sway. Water ripples on lakes.	19-24	29-38
6	Strong Breeze	Large branches sway. Umbrellas turn inside out.	25-31	39-49
7	Moderate Gale	Large trees sway. Walking is difficult.	32-38	50-61
8	Fresh Gale	Twigs break off trees. Walking is very difficult.	39-46	62-74
9	Strong Gale	Slight damage to houses and buildings.	47-54	75-88
10	Whole Gale	Trees are uprooted. Houses are damaged considerably.	55-63	89-102
11	Storm	Widespread damage.	64-73	103-117
12	Hurricane	Excessive damage and destruction.	More than 74	More than 117

Journal

Journal

_____

_____

_____

_____

_____

_____

_____

_____

_____

_____

_____

_____

_____

_____

_____

_____

_____

WEATHER

Extremes

TORNADO

What is it?

A tornado is a rapidly spinning cloud that is shaped like a funnel. Tornadoes start from severe thunderstorms. Winds come from different directions and cause the storm to spin. Air spins around what is called a vortex, or axis, of low pressure. Air from below is sucked up into the vortex, the air around it spins and a funnel cloud is formed which extends down from the storm cloud to the ground. Tornadoes can reach speeds of over 300 miles (483 km) per hour and they can do enormous damage. When a tornado is possible, there might be a dark green sky or large hail falling from the sky. The roaring noise of a tornado is sometimes compared to the sound of a freight train or a jet.

Amazing facts:

▷ Tornadoes can pick up entire buildings and toss them hundreds of yards away. They can destroy entire towns in minutes.

▷ Papers, letters, photographs and small items have been found as far as 200 miles (300 km) away from the sight of a tornado!

▷ In Great Bend, KS in 1915, a tornado destroyed a farm. The only survivors were 5 horses. The tornado had carried them a quarter mile from the barn. They were unhurt and still hitched to their post!

HURRICANE

What is it?

Hurricanes are known as the strongest storms on earth. They begin over the ocean as several small thunderstorms during the months when the ocean is the warmest. The storms come together and high tropical winds cause them to form a swirling circular pattern around a central "eye." They gain energy from the warm ocean waters and their power increases through the evaporation of seawater; which increases the speed of the spinning. Hurricanes are very deadly and costly storms that have nearly wiped out entire cities. Winds can reach speeds of 200 miles (322 km) per hour. Waves can reach a height of 20 feet (6 m) when they come ashore. This can cause disastrous flooding.

Amazing facts:

🌀 The energy of a hurricane is equal to 400 twenty-megaton hydrogen bombs.

🌀 Within the eye of the hurricane, it is clear and calm. People might think the storm is over, but they're mistaken because the storm is about to pass over again. The area surrounding the eye of the hurricane is the most powerful part of the storm.

🌀 Hurricanes used to be named by their locations, but that became confusing so they were given people's names.

DUST STORM

What is it?

A dust storm is when a strong wind blows a dense cloud of dust into the air. They happen in arid (desert) or semi-arid (prairie) climates when there has been little or no rain. A dust storm can affect an area as large as several hundred square miles. People contribute to dust storms with poor farming practices or overgrazing of livestock. The topsoil becomes dry and dusty and prone to blow away with a strong wind. During a dust storm, great clouds of dust can reduce visibility to zero making driving or just being outside dangerous.

Amazing facts:

🌀 Dust from dust storms in Africa or Asia has been blown all the way to North America. Miami, Fla., had amazing sunsets due to dust in the atmosphere caused by dust storms in the Sahara Desert.

🌀 A notorious decade of dust storms occurred in the U.S. in the 1930s during the Great Depression. They happened in parts of the Great Plains states in an area of the U.S. that came to be known as the Dust Bowl. Crops and farms were destroyed and buildings were sometimes buried in dust. This led to a great migration of people to California.

DROUGHT

What is it?

A drought is an extended period of time in which there is an unusually low level of precipitation in an area. Very hot temperatures also often accompany it. They generally last for only one season, but they can go on for years. When soil doesn't have enough water, it loses its ability to sustain nutrients and plants can't grow. Drought can lead to famine, forest fires, crop loss, soil erosion, dust storms, and lowered water levels in rivers and lakes. A drought can also lead to devastating economic loss. Droughts can have more of an economic impact than any other type of natural disaster.

Amazing facts:

☼ The Sahel region of Africa has experienced the longest drought in recent history. Parts of the Sahel are slowly turning to desert. Hundreds of thousands of people from this region have had to move or have died from famine.

☼ In the 1800s and early 1900s, people tried to make it rain by firing canons into the air.

What can you do?:

If you're in an area experiencing a drought, you should try to conserve water: take short showers, don't water lawns, and don't wash cars.

WEATHER Extremes

LIGHTNING

What is it?
When you see a bolt of lightning, you are seeing tiny particles called electrons moving through the air at great speeds. The electrons at the bottom of a storm cloud have a negative electrical charge. They're attracted to the positively charged electrons in the ground below or in trees, buildings—or sometimes people! The positively charged electrons on the ground reach up to join with the negatively charged electrons from the cloud and a lightning channel is formed. The electrons race through the channel so quickly, they make the air around them glow—and that's what you see when you see a bolt of lightning.

Amazing facts:
⚡Lightning can strike the same place more than once—the Empire State Building is struck many times every year.

⚡People sometimes die from lightning strikes, but about 80 percent of strike victims survive. One U.S. park ranger was struck 7 times over the course of 35 years—and survived them all!

⚡You can tell how far away lightning is by counting the seconds between the lightning flash and the thunder clap that follows. Five seconds equals one mile.

FLOOD

What is it?
A flood is when water overflows the banks of a river or some other body of water. Once the ground becomes saturated, water levels slowly rise. A flash flood is a fast and violent flood. Heavy rains falling in mountainous regions can cause water to flow down into valleys and canyons with a sudden and destructive force. Flash floods can also occur when a dam or levee breaks. Floods are very expensive disasters and they can take many lives.

Horrendous floods:
☁The worst flash flood in U.S. history occurred in Johnstown, Pa., in 1889. A dam broke, sending an entire lake of water—20 million tons (18 metric tons)—down onto the town below. The raging wall of water was 60 feet (12 m) high and it wiped away everything in its path—trees, houses, businesses, steel factories, trains and the people that were in the town. When it was over, more than 2,200 people had lost their lives.

☁The worst river flood in recorded history took place in 1887-88 in China. When the Yellow River overran its banks, hundreds of villages were destroyed and 900,000 people were killed. The flooded areas were equal in size to the entire state of Alabama.

BLIZZARD

What is it?
A blizzard is a storm which brings freezing temperatures, high winds, and lots of snow. They occur when 2 air masses collide. When a high-pressure cold front with freezing arctic air meets with a low-pressure air mass that has warm, moist air, the conditions are right for a blizzard.

What can happen:
✳In a blizzard, roads become slippery and visibility is low. The snow in the air can become so dense, it becomes impossible to see anything but white. This condition is called a whiteout. People can become disoriented in a whiteout and freeze to death because they can't find their way to shelter. People have been found frozen to death only steps away from their front doors!

✳The high winds and quickly falling snow in a blizzard can cause enormous drifts of snow which can reach over 50 feet and cover a building!

A disastrous blizzard:
In 1846, a group of 87 pioneers, known as the Donner Party, traveled through the mountains to California. They got caught in a fierce blizzard, which stranded them in a valley for the entire winter. They soon ran out of food and half of them died of starvation and disease.

GLOBAL WARMING

What is it?
Global warming is the gradual average increase in the Earth's temperature. It is a theory that temperatures will continue to rise because of an increase of gases in the Earth's atmosphere. These gases, called "greenhouse gases" cause heat to become trapped in our atmosphere in much the same way that heat is kept inside a greenhouse. The increase in these gases is caused by pollution.

What can happen:
No one knows for sure what will happen because of global warming. Some scientists think climates will change by the year 2100 and ecosystems will be disrupted, causing the extinction of many species of animals and plants. Glaciers will slowly melt. This would raise the sea levels, which would cause coastal flooding. Global warming would also cause more severe storms and drought.

What can you do?
✳Save electricity by turning lights or electrical appliances off when you're finished with them.

✳Ride your bike, walk, use public transportation, or car pool.

✳Recycle!

✳Plant trees—they use carbon dioxide, which is a greenhouse gas.